I0764249

REMINISCENCES

OF

CONGRESS.

BY

CHARLES W. MARCH.

NEW YORK:
BAKER AND SCRIBNER,
145 NASSAU STREET AND 36 PARK ROW.
1850.

C. W. BENEDICT,
Stereotyper and Printer,
201 William st.

PREFACE.

It was the original design of the author to have given a series of descriptive sketches of scenes and persons in Congress, unconnected with any antecedents or relations of the individuals introduced; but, finding on examination of what had been written that Mr. Webster formed the principal figure in each effort of his pen, he concluded to give the book a more personal character, and make it an approximation to a biography. This change of design will be detected in any, the most cursory, glance at the book; there being a want of congruity or unity too easily discernible throughout.

The writer need not say that he has not attempted a complete biography. It is difficult, if not absolutely impossible, to write the life of the living. It is not merely that friendship would be too partial, or enmity too censorious, to present a true estimate of the character and conduct of the person illustrated—the difficulty in obtaining correct information is greater during the life of a person, paradoxical as it may seem, than after his decease. When one eminent in life has gone down to the grave, numbers come forward with ambitious haste, some with letters, some with anecdotes, some with facts illustrative of the character and pursuits of the deceased, *and of their relationship to him.* The grief we feel at the departure of a distinguished friend is greatly mitigated by the public sympathy with our loss, and we hasten to give that sympathy a proper direction.

Besides, of what we gain as authentic, we are obliged to suppress a part; if not from regard to the feelings of the person, who is the subject of our memoir, yet from regard to the feelings of others whose relations with him might be affected unfavorably through our indiscreetness. There are many things told, in the intimacy of friendship, in the *abandon* of social intercourse, that it would be grossly reprehensible as well as indelicate to give publicity to.

The earlier part of Mr. Webster's life, rapidly sketched, it was thought, would lend new interest to his public career; —we like to trace greatness, if possible, to its seminal principle, and dwell upon its gradual development. The writer of these pages might have given a fuller account of this part of Mr. Webster's life, had he not been restrained by the fear of subjecting himself to a suspicion of having made too liberal use of the opportunities of private friendship. What has been given he hopes will prove not uninteresting.

NEW YORK, *July* 18*th*, 1850.

CONTENTS.

DANIEL WEBSTER.

CHAPTER I.

Daniel Webster was born on the 18th day of January, 1782, in the town of Salisbury, New Hampshire. His earliest ancestor, of whom the family has any certain knowledge, was Thomas Webster. He was settled in Hampton as early as 1636. The descent from him to Daniel Webster can be found recorded in the Church and Town Records of Hampton, Kingston, (now East Kingston) and Salisbury.

The family came originally from Scotland, two centuries ago and more. It is probable, however, from certain circumstances, that they tarried in England awhile, before emigrating to a new world. They did not bring over with them all the distinguishing peculiarities of their countrymen; the Scottish accent had become a mere tradition, in the time of Mr. Webster's father's father. The personal characteristics of the family are strongly marked: light complexions, sandy-hair in great profusion, bushy eyebrows, and slender rather than broad frames attest the Teutonic and common origin of the race. Dr. Noah Webster,—the compiler of the Dictionary,—was, in personal appearance, the *vera effigies* of the family.

The uncles of Daniel Webster had the same characteristics. They were fair-haired, and of rather slender form. His father, however, was of a different physical organization. No two persons could look like each other less than Ezekiel Webster—the father of Daniel—and either of his brothers. They resembled their father, who had the hereditary features and form; but Ezekiel Webster had the black hair, eyes, and complexion of his mother, whose maiden name was Bachelder. She was a descendant of the Rev. STEPHEN BACHELDER, a man famous in his time, in the County of Rockingham, and towns circumjacent. There are many persons now alive in Kingston, who will tell you they have heard their fathers say, she was a woman of uncommon strength of character, and sterling sense. Daniel and his only brother of the whole blood, Ezekiel, alone of the five sons of Ezekiel Webster, had the *Bachelder* complexion; the others ran off into the general characteristics of the race.

Many persons in Kingston and Salisbury still live who recollect Ebenezer Webster well. They say his personal appearance was striking. He was tall and erect; six feet in height; of a stalwart form, broad and full in the chest. His complexion was swarthy, features large and prominent: with a Roman nose, and eyes of a remarkable brilliancy. He had a military air and carriage,—the result, perhaps, of his service in the army. He enlisted, early in life, as a common soldier in the Provincial troops, and during the war of '56 served under Gen. Amherst, on the north-western frontier; accompanying that commander in the invasion of Canada. He attracted the attention and secured the good-will of his superior officers, by his faithful and gallant conduct; and before the close of the war, rose from the ranks to a captaincy. Peace between England and France soon following the capture of Quebec and conquest of Canada, the Provincial troops were disbanded, and returned to their homes.

Previous to the year 1763, the settlements in New Hampshire had made little or no progress towards the interior of the State, for more than half a century. The fitful irruptions of the French from Canada and the more constant if not more cruel assaults of their subsidized allies—the Indians—repressed any movement inward, into the country. To defend what they held, by a kind of *cordon militaire* of block-houses, was all the frontier-men hoped.

The session of Canada, however, to England, by the Treaty of Paris in 1763, removing the great obstacle to farther progress into the interior, the royal Governor of New Hampshire, BENNING WENTWORTH, began to make grants of townships in the central part of the State. Col. Stevens with some other persons about Kingston,—mostly retired soldiers,—obtained a grant of the township of Salisbury, then called, from the principal grantee, Stevens'-town. This town is situated exactly at the head-waters of the Merrimac River: which river is formed by the confluence of the Pemigiwasset and Winnipiseogee. Under this grant, Ebenezer Webster obtained a lot situate in the north part of the town. More adventurous than others of the company who obtained grants, he cut his way deeper into the wilderness, *making* the road he could not find. Here, in 1764, he built a log-cabin and lighted his fire. "The smoke of which," his son has since said on some public occasion, "ascended nearer the North Star than that of any of his majesty's New England subjects." His nearest civilized neighbor in the North was at Montreal, hundreds of miles off.

His first wife dying soon after his settlement at Salisbury, Ebenezer Webster married Abigail Eastman of Salisbury, a lady of Welsh extraction. She was the mother of Daniel and Ezekiel; and, like the mother of George Canning, was a woman of far more than ordinary intellect. She was proud of, and ambitious for her sons; and the distinction they both afterwards achieved, may have been, in part, at least, the result of her promptings. The mother knows better than any one the *mollia tempora fandi.* She knows what are words in season; when the mind is most ductile, and most capable of impressions intended to be permanent. If from our fathers we gain hardihood, mental or physical, and worldly wisdom, in all its variety, it is our mother, with her earnest, devoted, life-long love, that stimulates into healthy activity, whatever of good lies dormant in the heart; inspiring us to seek, if not for our own sake, for hers, honorable position, and an unequalled name.

Ebenezer Webster commemorated his second marriage, by the erection of a frame-house, hard by the log cabin. He dug a well near it, and planted an elm sapling. In this house, the subject of our memoir was born. The house has long since disappeared, from roof to foundation-stone. Nothing indicates its sometime existence but a cellar mostly filled up by stone and earth. But the well still remains, with water as pure, as cool, as limpid, as when first turned to the light: and will remain, in all probability, for ages, to refresh hereafter the votaries of genius, who make their pilgrimage hither to visit the cradle of one of her greatest sons. The elm that shaded the boy still flourishes in vigorous leaf, and may have an existence beyond its perishable nature. Like " the witch-elm that guards St. Fillan's Spring," it may live in story, long after leaf, and branch, and root have disappeared for ever.

It is a belief, I suspect almost universal, that natural scenery has great power over the development of character, moral and intellectual. That upon the impressionable mind of infancy, scenes, whether remarkable for traditionary interest, sublimity, ruggedness, or loveliness, stamp sensations of an indelible character; awaken, if they do not create, the poetic faculty. Burns, Byron, Burke, and Scott, are claimed by their several biographers as conclusive illustrations of the influence, picturesque nature exercises over the imagination and heart. The countless treasures of fancy and beauty, the high and solemn thoughts, the poetic fervor and luxuriant imagination which characterise, in a greater or less degree, the productions of these extraordinary men may have been suggested, or at least fully developed, by the striking features of the scenery, in the midst of which their earlier days were passed. The romantic localities of Ayr, the wild and picturesque scenery of the Highlands near Ballatrech, the rich, deep, and gorgeous views near by the old castle of Kilcolman—once the favorite residence of the poet Spenser—and the vicinity of Sandy Knowe, with its crags and cliffs, its ruined towers, and "mountains lone," severally the residences in early youth of Burns, Byron, Burke and Scott, may have given rise to feelings, which, increasing with earnest nourishment, till they became irrepressible from indulgence, found suitable expression afterwards in beautiful and nervous diction; in heroic verse, or glowing prose.

There is little softness or subdued expression in the features of the landscape round about Mr. Webster's birth-place. The bleak, harsh, stern hills, among which his cradle hung high in the air, like the eyrie of an eagle, are all untamed, untameable. But in their sadness, and deep but not voiceless solemnity, they are suggestive of lonely musings and thoughts original and lofty as themselves. They feed the hungry mind with images noble, elevated, and partaking of their own immortality. The laboring clouds in their vague career, often rested on the summits of these hills, covering them over as with a garment, so that they presented at times to the belated traveller of the valleys, the appearance of turbaned giants. Their scarred faces attested the violence of the tempests that ranged around them, and beat upon them. In winter, which lasted half the year, snows of a prodigious and dangerous depth covered the ground, obliterating every landmark, and giving to all nature an aspect of desolate sublimity. While, sometimes, in spring, a sudden and vast thaw would unloosen the embrace with which the snows held on to the mountains, and precipitate them in fearful volume, with the force and rush of the avalanche, into the valleys below; making of quiet streams mighty rivers, dangerous to ford or even approach; the crash of the pines in the woods, as they were borne to the earth by the superincumbent mass of snow, performing fit accompaniment to the scene.

In Mr. Webster's earliest youth an occurrence of such a nature took place, which affected him deeply at the time, and has dwelt in his memory ever since. There was a sudden and extraordinary rise in the Merimac River, in a spring thaw. A deluge of rain for two whole days poured down upon the houses. A mass of mingled water and snow rushed madly from the hills, inundating the fields far and wide. The highways were broken up, and rendered undistinguishable. There was no way for neighbors to interchange visits of condolence or necessity, save by boats, which came up to the very door-steps of the houses.

Many things of value were swept away, even things of bulk. A large barn, full fifty feet by twenty, crowded with hay and grain, sheep, chickens and turkeys, sailed majestically down the river, before the eyes of the astonished inhabitants; who, no little frightened, got ready to fly to the mountains, or construct another Ark.

The roar of waters, as they rushed over precipices, casting the foam and spray far above, the crashing of the forest-trees as the storm broke through them, the immense sea everywhere in range of the eye, the sublimity, even danger of the scene, made an indelible impression upon the mind of the youthful observer.

Occurrences and scenes like these excite the imaginative faculty, furnish material for proper thought, call into existence new emotions, give decision to character, and a purpose to action.

It was the great desire of Ebenezer Webster to give his children an education. A man of strong powers of mind and much practical knowledge himself, he still had felt deeply and often the want of early education, and wished to spare his sons the mortification he had experienced. The schoolmaster then was not abroad, at least had not visited Salisbury in his travels. Small town-schools there were, it is true, and persons superintending them called teachers—*lucus a non lucendo.* But these schools were not open half the year, and the schoolmasters had no claim to the position but their incapacity for anything else. Their qualification was their want of qualification. Reading and writing were all they professed, and more than they were able, to teach.

The school was migratory. When it was in the neighborhood of the Webster residence, it was easy to attend; but when it was removed into another part of the town, or another town, as was often the case, it was somewhat difficult. While Mr. Webster was quite young, he was daily sent two miles and a half or three miles to school, and, in the midst of winter, on foot. For carriages or carriage-roads then "were not;" and, with the exception of an occasional ride on horseback, he walked daily to school and back. If the school moved yet farther off, into a town not contiguous, his father boarded him out in a neighboring family. He was better provided with opportunities for obtaining whatever of instruction these schools could impart than his elder brothers, partly because he evinced early an irrepressible thirst for study and information, and partly because his father thought that his constitution was slender and somewhat frail—too much so for any robust occupation. But Joe, his elder half-brother, who was somewhat of a wag, used to say that "Dan was sent to school, in order that he might know as much as the other boys."

Mr. Webster had no sooner learnt to read, than he showed great eagerness for books. He devoured all he could lay hands upon. When he was unable to obtain new ones, he read the old ones over and over, till he had committed most of their contents to memory. Books were then (as Dr. Johnson said on some occasion) "like bread in a besieged town; every man might get a mouthful, but none a full meal." What were obtained, were husbanded with care. Owing chiefly to the exertions of Mr. Thompson, (the lawyer of the place,) of the clergyman, and Mr. Webster's father, a very small circulating library was purchased. These institutions about this time received an impetus from the zeal and labors of Dr. Belknap, the celebrated historian of New Hampshire.

Among the few books of the library, I have heard Mr. Webster say, he found the Spectator, and that he remembers turning over the leaves of Addison's Criticism upon Chevy Chase, for the sake of reading, connectedly, the ballad, the verses of which Addison quotes from time to time, as subjects of remark. "As Dr. Johnson said, in another case, the poet was read, and the critic neglected. I could not understand why it was necessary that the author of the Spectator should take so great pains to prove that Chevy Chase was a good story."

The simple, but sublime story of Chevy Chase, would be no indifferent test for the discovery of how much or how little of the poetic faculty there might be in an individual. None but those who had some poetic fervor could appreciate or even understand it: while those who felt its pathos, its beauty and grandeur most, needs must have the deepest sensibilities. A distinguished literary character has said that he would have been prouder to have been its author than of all the productions from which he derived his fame. Sir Philip Sydney said he never read it but his heart was stirred within him as at the sound of a trumpet.

Mr. Webster was early very fond of poetry. He was not satisfied with reading it merely, but committed a great deal to memory. The whole Essay on Man he could recite *verbatim* before he was fourteen years old. A habit of attentive exclusive devotion to the subject before him, aided by a wonderful memory, fixed everything deeply in his mind. It is this art, or talent, or genius, that works the miracles we read and behold. He had a great taste, too, for devotional poetry: Watts' Psalms and Hymns he committed to memory, not as a religious task, but as a pleasure. Nor was he less fond of, or less acquainted with, the sublime poetry of the Bible. Evidence of this is found everywhere in his works: for there is scarcely a speech or production of his that does not contain ideas or expressions, the types of which may be found in that book.

When he had attained his fourteenth year, his father took an important and decisive step with him. On the 25th day of May, 1796, Ebenezer Webster mounted his horse, put his son on another and proceeded with him to Exeter. He there placed him in Phillip's academy, then under the care of Dr. Benjamin Abbot, its well-known and respected President. The change was very great to a boy, who had never been from home before, and who now found himself among some ninety other boys,—a stranger among strangers,—all of whom had probably seen more of the world, and assumed to know so much more of it, than himself. But he was not long in reconciling himself to the change, and to his new duties. He was immediately put to English grammar, writing and arithmetic. A class-mate of his has informed me that he mastered the principles and philosophy of the first, between May and

October of that year; and that in the other studies he made respectable progress; in the autumn he commenced the study of the Latin language; his first exercises in which were recited to Joseph Stevens Buckminster, who was acting (in some college vacation, I think) as assistant to Dr. Abbott.

It may appear somewhat singular that the greatest orator of modern times should have evinced in his boyhood the strongest antipathy to public declamation. This fact, however, is established by his own words, which have recently appeared in print. "I believe," says Mr. Webster, "I made tolerable progress in most branches, which I attended to, while in this school; but there was one thing I could not do. I could not make a declamation. I could not speak before the school. The kind and excellent Buckminster sought especially to persuade me to perform the exercise of declamation, like other boys, but I could not do it. Many a piece did I commit to memory, and recite and rehearse in my own room, over and over again; yet when the day came, when the school collected to hear declamations, when my name was called, and I saw all eyes turned to my seat, I could not raise myself from it. Sometimes the instructors frowned, sometimes they smiled. Mr. Buckminster always pressed and entreated, most winningly, that I would venture. But I never could command sufficient resolution." Such diffidence of its own powers may be natural to genius, nervously fearful of being unable to reach that ideal which it proposes as the only full consummation of its wishes. It is fortunate, however, for the age, fortunate for all ages, that Mr. Webster by determined will and frequent trial overcame this moral incapacity—as his great prototype, the Grecian orator, subdued his physical defect.

He remained at the Exeter academy but a few months; accomplishing in these few months, however, the work of years to some. In February, 1797, his father placed him under the tuition of the Rev. Samuel Woods, in Boscawen; of whom his pupil always speaks in terms of affection and respect. He boarded in his family; and I have heard him say that Mr. Woods' whole charge for instruction, board, &c., was *but one dollar per week.* We pay much dearer now for much less.

It was on their way to the house of Mr. Woods that his father first opened to him his design of sending him to college—a purpose that seemed to him impossible to be fulfilled. It was so much more extravagant than his most extravagant hopes. It had never entertained his mind a moment. A collegiate education in those days was something of far greater importance than in these, when the ability to command it is so general. It made a marked man of thousands. It gave the fortunate graduate at once position and influence; and, if not genius, or eminent ability, supplied or concealed the want thereof. The alumnus surveyed life from an eminence, and could aspire to its chiefest honors by a kind of prescriptive right.

Most grateful to his father for the prospect held out through his self-sacrificing devotion, Mr. Webster applied himself to his studies with even increased ardor. All that Mr. Woods could teach he learnt. Among other books, he read Virgil and Cicero, both of whom he faithfully studied, the latter he warmly admired. Of the Latin classics, I presume, there is not one so familiarly known to Mr. Webster as Cicero. It may seem a little strange, indeed, that with all his early, eager, and constant study of Rome's greatest orator, he should not have imitated unconsciously his manner of expression or thought. He much more resembles Demosthenes, in vigor and terseness of expression, and in copious vehemence; whose works, in the meanwhile, he never so completely mastered.

At Boscawen, Mr. Webster was fortunate to find another circulating library, the volumes of which he fully appreciated. It was in this library, he met, for the first time, Don Quixote, in English. "I began to read it," (I have heard him say,) "and it is literally true that I never closed my eyes till I had finished it; nor did I lay it down any time for five minutes; so great was the power of this extraordinary book on my imagination."

In the summer of this year, August, 1797, he entered Dartmouth College, as a freshman.

His college life, it can be easily believed, was not an idle one. With such a desire for the acquisition of all kinds of knowledge, the danger to be apprehended was, he would undertake too much rather than too little; that his reading would be too miscellaneous, and that he would acquire, therefrom, habits of mental carelessness. From the testimony of his intimates in college, it is known that he read constantly.

Besides a regular attention to the prescribed studies of his class, he devoted himself to the acquisition of whatever was useful in English history, or graceful and becoming in English literature. He superintended also the publication of a little weekly newspaper, making selections for it from books and periodicals, and contributing, occasionally, an editorial of his own. These were, perhaps, the first of his productions ever published. I know not if they are to be met with now. He delivered some addresses while in college, before literary societies, which also were published.

Ezekiel Webster—the sole brother of Daniel of the whole blood—was destined by his father to remain at home and carry on the farm. But he had aspirations beyond this, and so had his brother for him. Accordingly, when Daniel returned home on a visit in his sophomore year, in the spring of '99, he held serious consultation with his brother Ezekiel, in relation to his wishes. It was resolved between them, that Ezekiel too should go to college, and that Daniel should be the organ of communication with their father on the subject. He lost no time in opening the negotiation, and experienced no great difficulty iu obtaining the consent of his father, who lived only for his children, to their design. The result was that in about ten days, Mr. Webster had gone back to college, having first seen his brother bid adieu to the farm, and place himself in school under a teacher in Latin. Soon afterwards Ezekiel went to Mr. Woods, and remained with him till he was fitted for college. In March, 1801, his father carried him to college, where he joined the Freshman class.

He had not great quickness of apprehension nor vivacity of intellect, and was not therefore early estimated at his full value. But he had a strong mind, great powers of observation, and memory. He acquired slowly but safely. Not fluent of speech, he was correct always in language and thought. Few excelled him in clearness or vigor of style, none in argumentative ability. He wanted but opportunity to have been a great man.

He fell dead, while arguing a cause in Concord, New Hampshire, in 1829. A handsome monument was erected to his memory in Boscawen, where he was buried.

Mr. Webster, while in college, during the winter vacations, kept school, to pay the collegiate expenses of his brother as well as his own. Being graduated in August, 1801, he immediately entered Mr. Thompson's office in Salisbury, as a student of law, and remained there till January following. The *res angusta domi* seemed then to require that he should go somewhere and do something to earn a little money. An application was at this time made to him from Fryeburg, Maine, to take charge of a school there. He accepted the offer, mounted his horse, and commenced his labors on reaching Fryeburg. His salary was $350 per annum, all of which he saved ; as he made besides a sum sufficient to pay his board and other necessary expenses, by acting as assistant to the Register of Deeds for the County, to whose chirography there was the one objection of illegibility. The *ache* is not yet out of his fingers —I have heard Mr. Webster say—which so much writing caused them.

In Fryeburg, he found also a circulating library, which he ran through. Here he borrowed and read for the first time Blackstone's Commentaries. Among other mental exercises, he committed to memory Mr. Ames' celebrated speech on the British Treaty.

In September, 1802, he returned to Mr. Thompson's office, in which he remained till February, 1804. Mr. Thompson was an excellent man and a respectable lawyer; but he did not understand how to make the study of the law either agreeable or instructive. He put his students to study after the old fashion, that is, the hardest books first. Coke's Littleton was the book in those days upon which pupils were broken in, —which is like teaching arithmetic, by beginning with diferential calculus. "A boy of twenty," says Mr. Webster, "with no previous knowledge on such subjects cannot understand Coke. It is folly to set him upon such an author. There are propositions in Coke so abstract, and distinctions so nice, and doctrines embracing so many conditions and qualifications, that it requires an effort not only of a mature mind, but of a mind both strong and mature, to understand him. Why disgust and discourage a boy by telling him he must break through into his profession through such a wall as this?"

Mr. Webster soon laid aside Coke till "a more convenient

season," and, in the meanwhile, took up other more plain, easy, and intelligible authors.

While not engaged in the study of the law, he occupied himself with the Latin classics. He added greatly to what acquisitions he had made in the language, while in college reading Sallust, Cæsar, and Horace. Some odes of the latter, which he translated into English, were published.

But books were not at this time of his life, as they never have been, Mr. Webster's sole study. He then was fond, and has been through life, of the manly field sports,—fishing, shooting and riding. These brought him into near communion with Nature and himself; supplied him with the material and opportunity for thought; made him contemplative, logical and earnest. At a subsequent period of his life, he found that the solitary rides he was wont to indulge in afforded him many an edifying day. The great argument in the Dartmouth College case was principally arranged in a tour he made from Boston to Barnstable and back. John Adams' speech before the Philadelphia Convention in '76, was composed by Mr. Webster, while taking a drive in a New England chaise. His favorite sport of angling gave him many a favorable opportunity for composition. The address for Bunker Hill (for instance) was all planned out even to many of its best passages, in *Marshpee Brook*;* the orator catching trout and elaborating sentences, at the same time.

* It is said—I know not upon what authority—that as the orator drew in some trout particularly large, he was heard to exclaim: "Ven-

A like fondness for solitary rambles and sequestered spots, is said to have characterized Canning and Burke; who found their fancies brighten and their philosophy invigorated by this self-communion. With them, as with the Roman Lawgiver, Egeria, avoiding crowds and bustling life, was to be met with only in solitude. So true is it that the intellectual man is never less alone than when alone; that to him his mind a kingdom is, and his own thoughts his most agreeable and instructive companions.

In July, 1804, Mr. Webster went to Boston, and, after some unsuccessful applications elsewhere, obtained admission as a student in the office of the Hon. Christopher Gore, who had then just returned from England, and resumed the practice of law. It was a most fortunate event for Mr. Webster. Mr. Gore was no less distinguished as a lawyer, than as a statesman and publicist,—eminent in each character,—and was besides one of the rare examples of the highest intellectual qualities united with sound, practical, keen common sense. He knew mankind no less than books; and the wisdom he derived from the study of both, he could impart, in most impressive language. With him Mr. Webster enjoyed the best op-

erable men! you have come down to us from a former generation. Heaven has bounteously lengthened out your lives, that you might behold this joyous day." As these identical sentences appeared afterwards in the Bunker-Hill Address, it would seem as if there was some plausibility for the story. At least, one can say with the Italian,—*Si non é vero, é bene trovato.*

portunity thus far of his life for studying books, and men, and things; and he made the best use of the opportunity. He attended the session of the Supreme Court which sat in August of this year, constantly, and reported all its decisions. He also reported the decisions of the Circuit Court of the United States. He read diligently and carefully the books, generally, of the Common and Municipal Law, and the best authorities on the Law of Nations, some of them for the third time, accompanying these studies with a vast variety of miscellaneous reading. His chief study, however, was the Common Law, and more especially that part of it which relates to the science of Special Pleading. This, one of the most ingenious and refined, and at the same time instructive and useful branches of the law, he pursued with constant devotion. Besides appropriating whatever he could of this part of the science from Viner, Bacon, and other books then in common study, he waded through Saunder's Reports—the old folio edition—and abstracted and put into English, out of the Latin and Norman-French, the pleadings, in all the reports. This undertaking, both as an exercise of the mind, and as an acquisition of useful learning, was of great advantage to him in his succeeding professional career.

An anecdote I have heard Mr. Webster tell in relation to his first interview with a gentleman, then and afterwards distinguished in the history of the country, it may not be improper to relate here. "I remember one day," says Mr. Webster, "as I was alone in the office, a man came in and asked for

Mr. Gore. Mr. Gore was out, and he sat down to wait for him. He was dressed in plain grey clothes. I went on with my book, till he asked me what I was reading, and, coming along up to the table, took the book and looked at it. 'Roccus,' said he, '*de navibus et nando.*' Well, I read that book too when I was a boy;' and proceeded to talk not only about 'ships and freights,' but insurance, prize, and other matters of maritime law, in a manner 'to put me up to all I knew,' and a good deal more. The grey-coated stranger turned out to be Mr. Rufus King.'

In March, 1805, Mr. Webster was admitted to practice, in the Suffolk Court of Common Pleas. The custom then prevailed for the patron to accompany his pupil into Court, introduce him to the Judges, make a brief speech in commendation of his studious conduct and attainments, and then move for his admission to the Bar. A person present on the occasion of Mr. Webster's admission, informs me that he remembers almost every word of Mr. Gore's speech, and that it contained, among other things, a prediction of his pupil's future professional distinction. In all probability the prediction, as is generally the case, aided its own accomplishment. Certainly, the favorable opinion of such a man as Mr. Gore must have been an additional incentive to Mr. Webster's ambitious hopes and efforts.

How much, after all, are the great men and events of history, apparently, the sport of accidents! The destiny of individuals, and no less of nations, seems not so much the result of foresight or determination, as of casual opinion or caprice ; or of circumstances, more uncertain than either. An adverse wind, neither to be anticipated nor overcome, kept the brewer's son within the shores of England, as he sought in a foreign clime the liberty of conscience refused him at home, and made him absolute master of his country's fortunes. An unsuccessful application for the Professorship of Logic in Glasgow University precipitated Edmund Burke upon his own energies, and gave to England its greatest philosophical orator. The offer of the clerkship of a county court, unexpected but not ungrateful, might, but for the earnest interposition of one man, have deprived America and the world of an intellect, of which neither America nor the world knows now the equal.

The clerk of the Court of Common Pleas for the county of Hillsborough, New Hampshire, resigned his office in January, 1805. Mr. Webster's father was one of the judges of this court ; and his colleagues, from regard for him, tendered his son the vacant clerkship. It was what Judge Webster had long desired. The office was worth $1500 per annum, which was in those days, and in that neighborhood, a competency ; or rather absolute wealth. Mr. Webster himself considered it a great prize, and was eager to accept it. He weighed the question in his mind. On the one side he saw immediate comfort ; on the other, at the best, a doubtful struggle. By its acceptance, he made sure his own good condition, and, what was nearer to his heart, that of his family. By its refusal, he condemned both himself and them to an uncertain, and probably, harrassing future. Whatever aspirations he might have cherished of professional distinction, he was willing cheerfully to relinquish, to promote the immediate welfare of those he held most dear.

But Mr. Gore peremptorily and vehemently interposed his dissent. He urged every argument against the purpose. He exposed its absurdity and its inconsequence. He appealed to the ambition of his pupil; once a clerk, he said, he always would be a clerk—there would be no step upwards. He attacked him, too, on the side of his family affection; telling him that he would be far more able to gratify his friends from his professional labors than in the clerkship. "Go on," he said, "and finish your studies; you are poor enough, but there are greater evils than poverty; live on no man's favor; what bread you do eat, let it be the bread of independence; pursue your profession; make yourself useful to your friends, and a little formidable to your enemies, and you have nothing to fear."

Diverted from his design by arguments like these, it still remained to Mr. Webster to acquaint his father with his determination, and satisfy him of its propriety. He felt this would be no easy task, as his father had set his heart so much upon the office; but he determined to go home immediately, and give him, in full, the reasons of his conduct.

It was mid-winter, and he looked round for a country sleigh—for stage-coaches, at that time, were things unknown in the centre of New Hampshire—and finding one that had come down to market, he took passage therein, and in two or three days was set down at his father's door. (The same journey is made now in four hours by steam.) It was evening when he arrived. I have heard him tell the story of the interview. His father was sitting before the fire, and received him with manifest joy. He looked feebler than he had ever appeared, but his countenance lighted up on seeing his *clerk* stand before him in good health and spirits. He lost no time in alluding to the great appointment—said how spontaneously it had been made—how kindly the chief justice proposed it, with what unanimity all assented, &c., &c. During this speech, it can be well imagined how embarrassed Mr. Webster felt, compelled, as he thought, from a conviction of duty to disappoint his father's sanguine expectations. Nevertheless, he commanded his countenance and voice, so as to reply in a sufficiently assured manner. He spoke gaily about the office ; expressed his great obligation to their Honors, and his intention to write them a most respectful letter ; if he could have consented to record anybody's judgments, he should have been proud to have recorded their Honors', &c., &c. He proceeded in this strain, till his father exhibited signs of amazement, it having occurred to him, finally, that his son might all the while be serious—"Do you intend to decline this office ?" he said at length. "Most certainly," replied his son ;"I cannot think of doing otherwise. I mean to use my tongue in the courts, not my pen ; to be an actor, not a register of other men's actions."

For a moment Judge Webster seemed angry. He rocked his chair slightly, a flash went over his eye, softened by age, but even then black as jet, but it immediately disappeared, and his countenance regained its usual serenity. Parental love and partiality could not after all but have been gratified with the son's devotion to an honorable and distinguished profession, and seeming confidence of success in it. "Well, my son," said Judge Webster finally, "your mother has always said that you would come to something or nothing, she was not sure which. I think you are now about settling that doubt for her." The judge never afterwards spoke to his son on the subject.

Mr. Webster having thus reconciled his father to his views returned to Boston. In March, following, having been admitted to the bar, as before stated, he went to Amherst, New Hampshire, where his father's court was then in session; from Amherst he went home with his father. His design had been to settle in the practice at Portsmouth; but unwilliug to leave his father, who had become infirm, and had no sons at home, he opened an office in Boscawen, near his father's residence, and commenced the practice of his profession.

Judge Webster lived but a year after his son's commencement of practice; long enough, however, to hear his first argument in court, and to be gratified with confident predictions of his future success. Then, like Simeon of old, he gathered up his garments and died.

He died in April, 1806. Exposure to the hardships of a

frontier life, more severe than we can now entertain any idea of, the privations and labors he suffered and underwent in the Indian wars, and the war of the Revolution, had broken in upon a constitution naturally robust, and hastened his decease. He was of a manly and generous character, and of a deportment and manner to gain him great consideration among all that knew him. In civil and military life, he obtained deserved distinction. Judge of the Court of Common Pleas for twelve or fourteen years, he made good, by the integrity of his purpose, the clearness of his judgment, and the strength of his character, the want of early education; and gained for his opinions and decisions a confidence and concurrence not always accorded to persons professionally more learned. He was distinguished also in his military career. Entering the army a private, he retired a major; and won his commission by faithful and gallant service, as well in the Revolutionary, as in the French and Indian wars. He acted as major under Stark, at Bennington, and contributed no little to the fortunate result of that day.

In May, 1807, Mr. Webster was admitted as attorney and counsellor of the Superior Court in New Hampshire, and in September of that year relinquished his office in Boscawen to his brother Ezekiel, who had then obtained admission to the bar, and moved to Portsmouth, according to his original intention.

He married in June, 1808, Grace Fletcher, the daughter of the Rev. Mr. Fletcher, of Hopkinton, N. H. By her he had four children; Grace, Fletcher, Julia and Edward; but one of whom, Fletcher, survives. Edward died with the army in Mexico, 1847, Major of the Massachusetts Regiment of Volunteers. He was one of the most gentlemanly, amiable, and honorable young men of the age.

Mr. Webster lived in Portsmouth nine years, wanting one month. The counsel most eminent at the bar of the county at that time, were Jeremiah Mason, Edward St. Loe Livermore, Jeremiah Smith, Judge of the Superior Court and Governor of the State; William King Atkinson, Attorney-General of the State; George Sullivan, also Attorney-General; Samuel Dexter and Joseph Story, of Massachusetts, all lawyers of much more than ordinary ability, and some of surpassing excellence. No bar, at that time, probably, in the country, presented such an array of various talents. Mr. Webster's estimate of Judge Story and Mr. Mason, expressed in public, will form not the least important nor least enduring monument to their fame. It will out last the sculptured marble. For Mr. Mason, his professional rival sometimes, his friend always, he entertained a warm regard as well as respect. Mr. Mason was of infinite advantage to him, Mr. Webster has said, in Portsmouth, not only by his unvarying friendship, but by the many good lessons he taught him, and the good example he set him in the commencement of his career. "If there be in the country a stronger intellect," Mr. Webster once said, "if there be a mind of more native resources, if there be a vision that sees quicker or sees deeper into whatever is intricate, or whatever is profound, I must confess I have not known it."

Mr. Webster's practice, while he lived in Portsmouth, was very much a circuit practice. He followed the Superior Court in most of the counties of the State, and was retained in nearly all the important causes. It is a fact somewhat singular of his professional life, that with the exception of instances in which he has been associated with the attorney-general of the United States for the time being, he has hardly appeared ten times as junior counsel. Once or twice with Mr. Mason, once or twice with Mr. Prescott, and with Mr. Hopkinson, are the only exceptions within recollection.

Mr. Webster's practice in New Hampshire was never lucrative. Clients then and there were not rich, and fees, consequently, were not large; nor were persons so litigious as in places less civilized by intelligence. Though his time was exclusively devoted to his profession, his practice never gave him more than a livelihood.

He never held office, popular or other, in the government of New Hampshire. He occasionally took part in political affairs, and was then not unfelt in his action. His vote was always given, his voice and pen sometimes exercised, in favor of the party whose principles he espoused. Even in that early period of his life, however, when something perhaps, could be pardoned to the vehemence of youth, he used no acrimonious language of his political opponents, nor suggested or participated in any act indicative of personal animosity towards them.

At thirty years of age, he had become well known and respected throughout the State ; so much so, that he was elected a Representative of the State in Congress, after an animated contest, in November, 1812, and took his seat at the extra session in May, 1813.

What has been written thus far, relates rather to the private life of Mr. Webster ; what follows concerns, mostly, his public ; as gathered from the records and contemporaneous testimony.

But the ingenuous youth of the country should understand, that Mr. Webster, great as he is, has not become so, without great study. Greatness has not been thrust upon him. He has studied books, he has studied mankind, he has studied himself, (which is the very fountain of all true wisdom,) deeply and conscientiously, from his earliest youth. There has been no unappropriated time with him ; none trifled away. Even in the hours of relaxation, he has thought of, and methodized the gleanings of the Past, or prepared results for the Future.

He laid early and solid the foundation of his fame. While the mind was eager and facile to receive earnest impressions, he sought after everything in the way of learning, that was sincere, elevated, and ennobling, to fill and satisfy it. He pursued no study he did not comprehend ; undertook no task to which he did not devote his whole mind. Whatever he strove after, he acquired, and whatever he acquired, he retained.

It was this early and constant seeking after knowledge—this desire unsatisfied with acquisition—this all-embracing pursuit, that determined his intellectual character, and prepared him for any encounter with the world. What he has said of Adams and Jefferson might be applied with equal truth to himself. "If we could now ascertain all the causes which gave them eminence and distinction, in the midst of the great men with whom they acted, we should find not among the least, their early acquisition in literature, the resources which it furnished, the promptitude and facility which it communicated, and the wide field it opened, for analogy and illustration; giving them, thus, on every subject, a larger view, and a broader range, as well for discussion, as for the government of their own conduct."

CHAPTER II.

The hall of debate is certainly not so dangerous as the battle-field. Life is not involved in its struggles; but still there can be perilled in it, no less, all that renders life desirable;—character, position, influence. These all may be staked upon the decision of the moment:

> "*Concurritur:*
> *Aut cita mors, aut victoria læta.*"

Moral and physical courage too are equally required in the one as in the other; there are many, indeed, who would prefer to lead a storming party or a forlorn hope, to undergoing the hazards of a forensic contest.

To Mr. Webster, a deliberative assembly was a scene of action entirely new. He had undergone, before his entrance into Congress, no preliminary training. The common schools of our orators—State Legislatures—he knew nothing of: all that he now saw resembled nothing he had ever seen. Yet he was neither perplexed, nor discouraged; he had subdued to a great degree his early diffidence, and became self-reliant. It may be said of him as it has been said of the younger Pitt;

the same composure, earnestness, and imposing manner, the same nervous, sinewy, accurate diction, the same variety, nicety and fullness of knowledge distinguished him on his first rising as in his later senatorial career.

But at Eton or Oxford, the future orators and statesmen of England are as regularly taught and drilled for the stations they are intended to fill, as pupils of the Polytechnic school. They have their mimic Parliament, where they acquire all the formula, the routine, and official etiquette—the *jus et norma loquendi*—which aid so much the success of their earliest efforts in the House. And when they enter Parliament, they but exchange the scene of their contests and their triumphs.

Mr. Webster was not like them "swaddled and rocked and dandled" into a Legislator. All he acquired was by dint of hard, unassisted labor. He had no models upon which to fashion himself. He had no example to encourage or warn. No one can read a speech of his, and not perceive the frequent and abundant evidence of obstacles encountered and overcome: of independent, manly thought; of early and close self-discipline; earnest introspection; great moral and intellectual hardihood.

He no sooner entered Congress than he obtained a commanding influence there; without hereditary name, official influence, or party ascendancy. His success was the result of a mind remarkably constituted for public effort; a mind that weighed and matured; that rejected nothing from prejudice, and embraced nothing without examination; that was full, sincere, logical, profound. It was, too, the result of an active, pertinacious diligence that has controlled his whole life.

He came into Congress in a period of great excitement. The insolent indifference of Great Britain to our maritime rights had provoked the country into a declaration of war, and hostilities were at this time at their height. It is true the measures of doubtful policy, which preceded the war, and its early injudicious management, had weakened in the minds of the people in various sections of the country the conviction of its justice or necessity. But in Congress, however, all the belligerent propositions of the administration were supported by decisive majorities. HENRY CLAY, who had urged the declaration of war with almost as much vehemence and pertinacity, as Cato the destruction of Carthage, was elected Speaker of the Lower House, by a triumphant vote, receiving eighty-nine out of one hundred and forty-eight ballots; and lent his position and great personal influence, in their whole extent, to the support of the policy of the administration.

Mr. Webster was placed on the Committee of Foreign Affairs. Though his reputation hitherto had been almost wholly provincial, whether from his personal deportment and appearance, some foreshadowings of his ability, or from some one of the many inexplicable causes that give to the judgment of man the certainty of intuition, this position was at once conceded to him. He was placed upon the most important Committee of the House, though one of the youngest (if not the youngest) Member in it, and wholly new to public affairs.

Besides the distinguished name of Clay, this Congress boasted others of a national character. CALHOUN, FORSYTH, GRUNDY, NATHANIEL MACON, WM. GASTON, of N. C.,—no less a jurist than a statesman,—TIMOTHY PICKERING, of Mass., JOHN W. TAYLOR, of New York, C. J. INGERSOLL, and WM. R. KING, then representing North Carolina, were all members of the House: most of them just starting, with generous rivalry, upon their race of distinction.

It was on Thursday, June 10th, 1813, that Mr. Webster made his maiden speech to the House. It was upon certain resolutions which he introduced in relation to the repeal of the Berlin and Milan Decrees, the first of which was in these words: "Resolved, That the President of the United States be requested to inform this House, unless the public interest should in his opinion forbid such communication, when and by whom, and in what manner, the first intelligence was given to this Government of the decree of the Government of France, bearing date the 28th of April, 1811, and purporting to be a definitive repeal of the Decrees of Berlin and Milan."

These resolutions were not introduced to embarrass the Administration, but to elicit information that might throw some light upon the proximate causes of the war, and enable members to best judge the most proper manner of conducting it.

Mr. Webster, in his speech on these resolutions displayed a cautious regard for facts, a philosophical moderation of tone, a fulness of knowledge, and an amplitude of historical illustration which astonished the House. There was no exaggeration of statement or argument, no sophistry nor uncalled-for rhetoric in his speech ; the oldest Parliamentarian could not have exhibited more propriety and decency of manner or language, nor the most able, a logic more perspicacious or more convincing. There was a harmony between his thought and its expression, that won attention and compelled admiration. The opening of his speech was simple, unaffected, without pretension, gradually gaining the confidence of his audience by its transparent sincerity and freedom from aught resembling display. As the orator continued and grew animated, his words became more fluent, and his language more nervous ; a crowd of thoughts seemed rushing upon him, all eager for utterance. He held them, however, under the command of his mind, as greyhounds with a leash, till he neared the close of his speech, when, warmed by the previous restraint, he poured them all forth, one after another, in glowing language.

The speech took the House by surprise, not so much from its eloquence as from the vast amount of historical knowledge and illustrative ability displayed in it. How a person, untrained to forensic contests and unused to public affairs, could exhibit so much Parliamentary tact, such nice appreciation of the difficulties of a difficult question, and such quiet facility in surmounting them, puzzled the mind. The age and inexperience of the speaker had prepared the House for no such display, and astonishment for a time subdued the expression of its admiration.

"No member before," says a person then in the House, "ever rivetted the attention of the House so closely, in his first speech. Members left their seats where they could not see the speaker, face to face, and sat down, or stood on the floor, fronting him. All listened attentively and silently, during the whole speech; and when it was over, many went up and warmly congratulated the orator; among whom, were some, not the most niggard of their compliments, who most dissented from the views he had expressed."

Chief Justice Marshall, writing to a friend sometime after this speech, says: "at the time when this speech was delivered, I did not know Mr. Webster, but I was so much struck with it, that I did not hesitate then to state, that Mr. Webster was a very able man, and would become one of the very first statesmen in America, and perhaps the very first."

The speech immediately raised its author to the first consideration in the House, and gained him great reputation throughout the country. The object it proposed was merely information respecting the time and manner in which the revocation of the Berlin and Milan Decrees reached the President. Certain opponents, however, of the administration used the introduction of the resolutions as an opportunity for assault upon it, particularly as related to its conduct of the war. The National Intelligencer,—the organ of the dominant party,—says in the paper of June 18th: "This debate has now assumed such a character, that, although there is but little opposition to Mr. Webster's motion, it has become necessary for the advocates of the present war, for the friends of the administration, the defenders of their country's reputation, to repel the violence of their opponents, and in turn pursue to the inmost recesses of their coverts, and drag them forth into the light of day."

But Mr. Webster took no part in the debate after it had assumed a factious character; his object being, not to foment party quarrels, but to carry out a national purpose.

His resolutions were carried by a large majority; the first, by a vote of 137 to 26; and President Madison, in obedience to the call of the House, communicated full and satisfactory information upon the subject.

Mr. Webster was not in Congress when the war with Great Britain was commenced, nor in public life. As a private citizen, he entertained opinions adverse to the policy of the restrictive system and the embargo, considering them more injurious in their operation to our own country than to England; and in this opinion, Mr. Calhoun and other prominent members of the Republican party concurred.

When he entered Congress, war was raging. He did not always approve either in his speeches or by his votes the manner in which it was carried on; but he never refused his vote to any measure for defending the country, repelling invasion, or giving greater force and vitality to the laws. He was not unmindful that his father had fought the same enemy in our revolutionary struggle; nor would he himself have hesitated to take the field, had the country needed his arm. Portsmouth—the town of his residence—being threatened with attack from a fleet of the enemy, hovering over the coast, he was placed, on the nomination of JOHN LANGDON, a man of odorous patriotism, at the head of the committee raised for its defence.

The best way of annoying England, and crippling its energies was, he thought, by attacking her on the sea. Before he was elected to Congress, and before war, though threatening, had been declared, he put forth some vigorous articles in favor of the navy; and he had no sooner entered the House, than he raised his voice to urge a greater attention to the character and equipment of this gallant service. "We were at war," he said afterwards, "with the greatest maritime power on earth. England had gained an ascendancy on the seas over the whole combined force of Europe. She had been at war twenty years. She had tried her fortunes on the Continent, but generally with no success. At one time, the whole Continent had been closed against her. A long line of armed exterior, an unbroken hostile array, frowned upon her from the Gulf of Archangel, round the promontory of Spain and Portugal, to the foot of the boot of Italy. There was not a port which an English ship could enter. Everywhere on the land the genius of her great enemy had triumphed. He had defeated armies, crushed coalitions, and overturned thrones; but like the fabled giant, he was unconquerable only when he touched the land. On the ocean he was powerless. That field of fame was his adversary's, and her meteor flag was streaming in triumph all over it.

"To her maritime ascendancy England owed everything, and we were at war with her. One of the most charming of her poets has said of her, that

'Her march is o'er the mountain wave,
Her home is on the deep.'——

"Now since we were at war with her, I was for intercepting this march; I was for calling upon her, and paying our respects to her at home; I was for giving her to know that we, too, had a right of way over the seas, and that our marine officers and our sailors were not entire strangers on the bosom of the deep; I was for doing something more with our navy than to keep it on our shores for the protection of our own coasts and our own harbors; I was for giving play to its gallant and burning spirit; for allowing it to go forth upon the seas, and encounter, on an open and equal field, whatever the proudest and the bravest of the enemy could bring against it. I knew the character of its officers, and the spirit of its seamen; and I knew that, in their hands, though the flag of the country might go down to the bottom, while they went with it, yet that it could never be dishonored or disgraced."

The speech he delivered in favor of putting the navy in proper condition, and sending it forth to gain laurels on a free, open field, was one of the best he made during the session.

A quarter of a century after the war, Mr. Calhoun, in the Senate of the United States, in some reply to Mr. Webster, made a general allusion to his votes and speeches during the war, and insinuated that they might not all bear scrutiny. Mr. Webster, after indignantly repelling the charge, and proving its groundlessness, concluded in these words: "As I do not mean to recur to this subject often, or ever, unless indispensably necessary, I repeat the demand for any charge, any accusation, any allegation whatever, that throws me behind the honorable gentleman, or behind any other man, in honor, in fidelity, in devoted love to that country in which I was born, which has honored me, and which I serve. I who seldom deal in defiance, now, here, in my place, boldly defy the honorable member to put his insinuation in the form of a charge, and to support that charge by any proof whatever."

The challenge thus thrown out, Mr. Calhoun never accepted, nor, is it probable, any other man ever will.

The principal speeches made by Mr. Webster during this Congress, were upon his own resolutions—upon the increase of the Navy—upon the rescinding of the Embargo, and upon the Previous Question; all indicative of various as well as eminent talent.

In January, 1814, while Mr. Webster was in Washington attending to his duties as a member of Congress, a great fire took place in Portsmouth—in which he lost house, furniture, books, everything—a loss to him, at that time of no inconsiderable magnitude.*

* This was the "Great Fire" of Portsmouth. I have heard Mr

In the beginning of the year 1814, John Quincy Adams, then minister to Russia, James A. Bayard, of Delaware, Jonathan Russell, of R. I., and Henry Clay, were appointed Commissioners to Gottenburg, to meet the Commissioners of Great Britain under an overture proposed by the government of that country and accepted by ours, for concerting the conditions of peace between the two countries.

Webster tell an anecdote relating to the burning of his house, which it may be worth while to repeat.

The house was the first to catch on fire. It took fire on the roof—as was supposed, from a neighboring stable. No one was at home but Mrs. Webster, her daughter Grace, and the servants—Fletcher being out at nurse. A man by the name of Parry—an acquaintance—rushed into the house, and seizing Mrs. Webster by the hands exclaimed: "Mrs. Webster, don't be agitated—don't be alarmed, Mrs. Webster." "I am not alarmed, Mr. Parry. Why should I be? What's the matter?" "Don't be alarmed, Mrs. Webster—for Heaven's sake, don't be alarmed," cried he—"there is no danger." "Danger of what?" said Mrs. Webster—"What *is* the matter, Mr. Parry?" "My dear madam don't be alarmed, *but your house is all on fire, and the roof must be falling in by this time.*"

Mrs. Webster, with great presence of mind, gave directions for saving whatever of the furniture, &c., was easy of access and removal; some of the neighbors hastening in to aid her. But they, however, were obliged to leave her to take care of their own houses, which were soon likewise in a blaze—many houses, and property to a large amount, were destroyed.

Mr. Webster had been diverted from his purpose of insuring house and furniture, and suffered in consequence a total loss, with the exceptioe of the few articles preserved by his wife, of both—in all, perhaps, $7,000.

The acceptance of this mission by Mr. Clay necessarily vacated the Speakership. On January 19th, he resigned the office, with these remarks:

"Gentlemen,—I have attended you to-day, to announce my resignation of the distinguished station in this House, with which I have been honored by your kindness. In taking leave of you, gentlemen, I shall be excused for embracing this last occasion, to express to you personally my thanks for the frank and liberal support, the chair has experienced at your hands. Wherever I may go, in whatever situation I may be placed, I can never cease to cherish, with the fondest remembrance, the sentiments of esteem and respect with which you have inspired me."

Certainly, no one ever presided over any deliberative body, in this country, with more personal popularity and influence than Mr. Clay. He governed the House with more absoluteness than any Speaker that preceded or followed him. It was a power founded upon character and manners. Fearless, energetic, decided, he swayed the timid by superior will, and governed the bold, through sympathy. A chivalric bearing, easy address, and a warm manner that seemed to imply a warm heart, drew around him crowds of admirers. He cultivated—what our great men too much neglect—the philosophy of manners. None knew better than he the wondrous power in seeming trifles; how much a word, a tone, a look can accomplish; what direction give to the whole character of opinion and conduct. There seemed nothing constrained in his courtesy, nothing simulated; all his manner was simple, unaffected, ardent; if it were not genuine, he had early arrived at the perfection of art, and concealed the art.

As an orator, he was unequalled; even in an assembly that boasted of Cheves, of Lowndes, of Forsyth, and others no less distinguished. His voice was sonorous and musical, falling with proper cadence from the highest to the lowest tones; at times, when in narrative or description, modulated, smooth and pleasing, like sounds of running water; but when raised to animate and cheer, it was as clear and spirit-stirring as the notes of a clarion, the House all the while ringing with its melody.

Oftentimes he left his chair to address the House. A call of the House would not have brought members in more eagerly. Few, indeed, could have indulged in such frequency of speech, and retained personal ascendency. But his influence seemed to increase in strength, the oftener it was exerted. He had a wonderful tact, by which he judged, as by intuition, when the subject, or the patience of his audience, threatened to be exhausted; and took care always to leave the curiosity of his hearers unsatisfied.

"I was a member of the House during the war," writes a gentleman to the editor of these papers, "and was present when Mr. Clay made his farewell speech on resigning the Speakership. It was an impressive occasion. Not only were all the seats of members occupied, but many senators attended, and a large miscellaneous crowd. The war which he had been most active in hastening, and most energetic in prosecuting, he was now commissioned with others to close. He was the youngest of the Commissioners, but sagacious far beyond his years. The hopes of the country tired of a protracted struggle, grew brighter from his appointment.

"Undoubtedly, at this time, even in his youthful age, he had no rival in popularity. His name was everywhere familiar as "household words." His own bearing evinced a consciousness of his favor in the country. I was struck with his appearance on this occasion. There was a fire in his eye, an elation in his countenance, a buoyancy in his whole action, that seemed the self-consciousness of coming greatness. Hope brightened, and joy elevated his crest. As full of confidence, gallant bearing, and gratified look, he took his seat in the Speaker's chair, his towering height even more conspicuous than usual, I could not but call to mind Vernon's description of Henry, Prince of Wales, in Shakspeare:

"I saw young Harry, with his beaver on,
His cuisses on his thigh, gallantly armed,
Rise from the ground, like feather'd Mercury,
And vaulted with such ease into his seat,
As if an angel dropp'd down from the clouds,
To turn and wind a fiery Pegasus,
And witch the world with noble horsemanship.

"Age at this time had not withered, nor custom staled the infinite variety of his genius. The defects of his character had not been developed; prosperity had not sunned them;

and they lie unsprouted in his heart; nor had he committed any of the blunders of his later life, which, in a political view, have been pronounced worse than crimes.

"After he had resigned the chair, in a neat and appropriate speech, he came down to the floor; and members surrounded him, to express their great grief at his withdrawal,—mingled, however, with congratulations upon his appointment, and with the expression of sanguine anticipations of the success of his mission."

Mr Clay having resigned his seat, with the remarks already quoted, Mr. Findley, of Pennsylvania, moved the following resolution:

"*Resolved*, That the thanks of this House be presented to Henry Clay, in testimony of their approbation of his conduct, in the arduous and important duties assigned to him as Speaker of the House."

This resolution was carried by a vote of 144 to 9. "The minority on this occasion," says the National Intelligencer, "was composed of those whose approbation, we may venture to say, Henry Clay never courted, if he desired it."

On the retirement of Mr. Clay, Langdon Cheves, of South Carolina, was elected Speaker, and performed the duties of the office with great ability.

Much intellectual sparring took place this session between Calhoun, Lowndes, Forsyth and Cheves, on one side, and Webster, Pickering and Oakley on the other. The almost life-long contest between Calhoun and Webster had its origin then. They have differed on measures and principles, but chiefly upon the construction of the Constitution, at least in later years. Earlier in life, Mr. Calhoun contended with as much force and eloquence for a liberal construction of this instrument, as, later, for a narrow one.

But Mr. Calhoun and Mr. Webster never infused into their political controversies the bitterness of personal feeling. Each was too great to feel envious of the other's ability, too magnanimous to withhold admiration of the other's extraordinary endowments. Never, during their whole Parliamentary career, did either of these distinguished gentlemen, on any occasion, impugn the other's motives, or address him in words of unkindness. They respected each other, and they respected themselves.

The eminence Mr. Webster rose to, even in this his first parliamentary term, was generally acknowledged even by his political opponents. Mr. Lowndes, who was one of the very few who could have disputed his rank, said of him: "The North had not his equal, nor the South his superior."

Mr. Webster was re-elected to Congress from New Hampshire, in August, 1814, after a warm political canvass.

Early in January, 1815, Mr. Dallas, of Pennsylvania, introduced into the House a bill for the charter of an United States Bank. This measure Mr. Webster opposed in a speech of great force, displaying an amount of knowledge of the history and philosophy of finance, which astonished even those who thought most highly of his abilities. He denounced it as a mere paper bank—a mere machine for fabricating irredeemable paper—a plan for using the sanction of the Government to defraud the people.* Mr. Calhoun also opposed it, and Mr.

* "What sort of an institution, Mr. Speaker," said he, "is this? It looks less like a bank than a department of Government. It will be properly the paper-money department. Its capital is Government debts the amount of its issues will depend on Government necessities; Government, in effect, absolves itself from its own debts to the bank, and, by way of compensation, absolves the bank from its own contracts with others. This is, indeed, a wonderful scheme of finance. The Government is to grow rich, because it is to borrow without the obligation of repaying, and is to borrow of a bank which issues paper without liability to redeem it. If this bank, like other institutions which dull and plodding sense has erected, were to pay its debts, it must have some limits to its issues of paper, and, therefore, there would be a point beyond which it could not make loans to Government. This would fall short of the wishes of the contrivers of this system. They provide for an unlimited issue of paper, in an entire exemption from payment. They found their bank, in the first place, on the discredit of Government, and then hope to enrich Government out of the insolvency of their bank. With them, poverty itself is the main source of supply, and bankruptcy a mine of inexhaustible treasure. They rely, not in the ability of the bank, but in its beggary; not in gold and silver collected in its vaults, to pay its debts and fulfil its promises, but in its locks and bars, provided by statute, to fasten its doors against the solicitations and clamors of unfortunate creditors. Such an institution, they flatter themselves, will not only be able to sustain itself, but to buoy up the sinking credit of the Government. A bank which does not pay, is to guaranty the engagements of a Government which does not pay! Thus the empty vaults of the treasury are

Lowndes, in able speeches, and led off against the measure some twenty members of the Republican party. It was lost, after a severe struggle, by the casting vote of the Speaker, Mr. Cheves, of S. C.

It was, however, reconsidered, and amended in several important particulars. The bill, as amended, passed the House by a large majority, Mr. Webster voting in its favor. It passed the Senate, but not without much difficulty, and was sent to the President, who returned it to the House where it originated, with his reasons for refusing to sign it, the principal of which was its inexpediency. An attempt to pass it—the veto notwithstanding—failed entirely.

On the 8th day of January, of this year, was fought the ever-memorable battle of New Orleans, the result of which spread joy and exultation throughout the nation. The heroic conduct of Gen. Jackson was the praise of every tongue ; no encomium seemed equal to his merits. Congress, responding to the grateful feeling of the nation, voted him thanks and medals, in commemoration of his gallant services.* The victory was fit copestone to the war.

to be filled from the equally empty vaults of the bank, and the ingenious invention of a partnership between insolvents is to restore and establish the credit of both."

* Henry Clay said, in his speech to the House, in March, 1816 : "Whilst the Mississippi continues to bear the tributes of the Iron Mountains and the Alleghany to her Delta and to her Gulf of Mexico, the 8th of January shall be remembered, and the glory of that day shall stimulate

The thirteenth Congress adjourned on the 4th of March, 1815, the date of its constitutional existence. Mr. Webster returned to New Hampshire, and his professional avocations, keeping company with judges, sheriffs and witnesses, plaintiffs and defendants. He began at this time to agitate the question of change of residence, his practice in New Hampshire ceasing to afford him a proper livelihood. His mind hesitated between Albany and Boston ; till, finally, being unable to make an immediate election between the two places, he postponed, for a later period, the determination of the question.

On the re-assembling of Congress in December, 1815, Henry Clay was again elected Speaker, no one of his party contesting his candidatecy. He was welcomed back to the seat in which he had gained such eminent distinction. His popularity in the country had nearly reached its culminating point. Peace with Great Britain, which the heart of the people longed for now, as before for the declaration of war, had been satisfactorily arranged, and partly through his agency ; and the multitude, ever seeking some tangible object of worship, lavished upon him every expression of grateful feeling and personal devotion. He was associated in their minds with the national glory and national prosperity. All the Government had proposed by waging war against Great Britain—the freedom of our commerce, the safety of our seamen, and the honor of our flag,—had been secured, if not by express condition in

future patriots, and nerve the arms of unborn freemen in driving the presumptuous invader from our country's soil."

the Treaty of Peace, yet by the readiness with which the war had been entered upon, the earnestness with which it had been carried on, and its ultimate success. Those, therefore, who had been most warm for the declaration of war, and most active in its vigorous prosecution, were now most endeared to the hearts of the nation.

Mr. Calhoun appeared in this session as the great champion of a National Bank, a Protective Tariff, and Internal Improvements. In relation to the Tariff, he said in his well-considered speech of April, 1816: "In regard to the question how far manufactures ought to be encouraged, it was the duty of this Government, as a means of defence, to encourage domestic industry, more especially that part of it which provides the necessary materials for clothing and defence.

"The question relating to manufactures, must not depend on the abstract principle, that industry left to pursue its own course, will find in its own interest all the encouragement that is necessary. I lay the claims of the manufacturer entirely out of view; but on general principles, without regard to their interest, a certain encouragement should be extended, at least to our woollen and cotton manufactures."

Mr. Calhoun was the architect of the tariff of 1816. But for his exertions and South Carolina votes, it had never passed. Even the *minimum*, the object afterwards of so much reviling and wrathful rhetoric on the part of the South, was established by Southern votes; and the *principle* of protection advocated, urged, and secured.

Mr. Webster disagreed with Mr. Calhoun, and opposed the high tariff policy. The bill that finally passed was amended, on his motion, in certain important particulars; on its passage, however, he voted against it, as being crude in its character, and certain to be injurious in its operation to his constituents. It has been said that at one time Mr. Webster denied the constitutional power of Congress to impose a tariff for protection. Such is not the case. It is true, however, that in a speech at Faneuil Hall, sometime in 1820, he contended that if the power of protection be inferred only from the revenue power, the protection could only be incidental; that duties ought not be laid for the mere object of protection.

But Mr. Madison's published opinion, after this period, and his declaration that the Convention which framed the Constitution did intend to grant the power of protection, *under the commercial clause*, were conclusive, in Mr. Webster's judgment, of the power. And the *policy* of the tariff having become the settled and established policy of the country, he acquiesced in and supported it.

In his speech against chartering the Bank of the United States, which he delivered in February, '16, Mr. Webster displayed an amount of financial knowledge, which surprised the House no less than his acquaintance with the history and policy of other countries, as made known to Congress in his speech two years before. His mind grasped all the details, as well as the more prominent principles of the financial system, and defined them clearly to his audience. He introduced amendments restrictive of the powers and privileges of the bank, which he carried through by his earnest argument of their necessity; among others, one which made it compulsory and penal on the bank to pay its *deposits* in specie, as well as its notes and bills; and another, limiting the right of the institution to sue, in State Courts alone, instead of "all courts whatsoever," as provided for in the original bill.

He disliked, and protested against, the participations of the government in the direction and management of the bank,—contending it would be alike injurious to both parties; and urged, with much vehemence of argument, other fatal objections to the bill.

But it passed the House by a vote of 82 to 61. John Randolph, with other republicans, less distinguished, voting in the negative.

Mr. Calhoun too, was the father of the system of National Improvements. Early in the next session of Congress—in December, 1816—a committee was raised on his motion, of which he was appointed chairman, to consider the propriety of setting apart the *bonus*, which the Bank of the United States paid for its charter, amounting to one million five hundred thousand dollars, and also the dividends in the stock of the Bank belonging to the United States, as a permanent fund for internal improvements; and, soon after, reported a bill for carrying out the objects for which the committee had been appointed.

In the Committee of the Whole House on this bill, he made a very able, argumentative speech on the general policy of national improvements, and the power of Congress over the subject.

" Let us make," says he, " permanent roads, not like the Romans, with the view of subjecting and ruling provinces, but for the more honorable purposes of defence, and connecting more closely the interests of various sections of this great country.

" Let us bind the Republic together, with a perfect system of roads and canals. Let us conquer space. It is thus the most distant parts of the Republic will be brought within a few days travel of the centre ; it is thus that a citizen of the West will read the news of Boston still moist from the press."

In truth, no one member of this celebrated fourteenth Congress, acquired more national reputation than Mr. Calhoun. His early parliamentary career gave promise of permanent utility to the whole country. The liberality of his views, the earnestness and ability with which they were expressed, and the sympathy and co-operation with which they were met, gave assurance to the country of a prosperous Future.

Men watched his star rising in the clear unclouded sky, and rejoiced, for they thought to see it bring in its train national health, happiness and greatness. A Southerner by birth, he expressed and advocated no local views ; but, with a mind as vast as its interests, embraced in his language and his action, the whole country. His popularity was, as his views, national; in Massachussetts he was no less regarded than in South Carolina; his name was familiarized everywhere.

He soon after became a member of Mr. Munroe's cabinet; and, in that position, lent new force to the policy he had so warmly advocated while in Congress. In fact, by this time, his congressional and ministerial services had determined the minds of many influential politicians in various sections of the country, to bring him out as the most proper candidate for the presidency. In the North, he was especially a favorite. His efficient advocacy of internal improvements, sound currency, and protection of domestic manufactures, had gained him a strong alliance there. Mr. Webster, among others, was not insensible either to his services, or to the popularity they had justly given him; and he advised a young friend of his, then editing a paper in one of the New England States, and who had sought his views in regard to the proper candidate of the North for the presidency in the approaching campaign, (1824,) to support Mr. Calhoun for the position; unfortunately, a short-sighted, narrow, sectional pride of feeling induced New England to give its vote to John Quincy Adams, whose elevation, by a seeming retributive justice, did more to render New England men, measures and views unpopular, than any other political event could possibly have done. New England has never recovered from this untoward event.

At the close of the fourteenth Congress, the three names

most distinguished in it—WEBSTER, CLAY, CALHOUN—occupied, almost exclusively, the minds of all men. There was nothing, seemingly, beyond the scope of their ambition or attainment. They had but to form a triumvirate, and divide the world between them; not in contemporaneous but alternate fruition. Had they done so, the historian of the twenty-four years in which they should have filled the presidential chair would have described an era of national honor, national prosperity, and national greatness, the like of which, in no country, have the records of ancient or modern times afforded. The imagination halts in the vain attempt to reach the comprehension of such an ideal, and turns unsatisfied away.

The devoted friends of these eminent men might be equally unwilling and unable to say, whose hot ambition of the three prevented such a glorious consummation; in after times, however, the impartial historian, reviewing carefully their character and conduct, may discover, and demonstrate to the world, the one most faithless to the present, and all future ages.

After the adjournment of Congress, in August, 1816, Mr. Webster left Portsmouth, New Hampshire, and established his residence in Boston. His professional practice in New Hampshire had ceased to afford him and his family a livelihood, broken in upon, as it was, by his duties at Washington. In Boston, his name as an advocate and orator was, by this time well known; and influential friends there succeeded in prevailing upon him to select that city for his future home.

He never has since gone into a New Hampshire court, except on one occasion, when he went down from Boston in September, 1817, in the Dartmouth College case.

The question in this case was—whether certain acts of the New Hampshire Legislature, purporting to *enlarge* and *improve* the Corporation of Darmouth College, and *amend* its charter, were binding upon the Corporation, without their acceptance or assent; and not repugnant to the Constitution of the United States? Mr. Webster argued the case as counsel for the Corporation. The opinion of the Superior Court of the State, before which it was argued, as delivered by Chief Justice Richardson, was in favor of the validity and constitutionality of the acts; and judgment was entered accordingly.

Whereupon a writ of error was sued out by the Corporation of the College to remove the cause to the Supreme Court of the United States. It came on for argument there in March, 1818, and before all the judges. It was argued by Mr. Webster and Mr. Hopkinson for the plaintiffs in error, and by Mr. Holmes and the Attorney-General, for the other side.

The question involved in this case was quite new to our jurisprudence; and when the case had been called up for argument, and Mr. Justice Story had run his eye over it, he said he did not see how anything could be made out of it.

He changed his opinion on the hearing of Mr. Webster's argument, and coincided with his colleagues in declaring the acts of the Legislature unconstitutional and invalid, and in reversing the judgment of the State Court.*

This may be called Mr. Webster's first constitutional argument; and in this view alone would be sufficient to provoke its careful study; even if it did not embrace the clearest, yet most succinct account of eleemosynary corporations, of their character and purposes, their privileges, property and immunities, ever expressed in words. No case, however remotely connected with it in principle, has since been argued, or ever will be, but with liberal quotations of its language and opinions.

When Mr. Webster removed to Boston, he had still one session to serve as member of Congress from New Hampshire. It was a session of no great importance to Mr. Webster's per-

* From the security gained to the chartered privileges of this corporation by Mr. Webster, through this final decision of the Supreme Court of the United States, he is entitled to be considered the second founder of the institution. He far more than repaid by his success all he obtained from his collegiate education. His name should be held in grateful commemoration there, in all coming ages, no less than that of Henry VI. at Eton:

> "Where grateful science still adores
> Her holy Henry's shade."

It is no little creditable in the mean time, to the character of New Hampshire, that its Legislature and citizens generally, rendered an immediate if not cheerful obedience to the decision of the highest tribunal known to the constitution. But New Hampshire ever was a law-abiding and authority-regarding State.

sonal history, or to the country. No agitating questions were brought before it, either of domestic or foreign character; and legislation was moderate and unimpeded.

A domestic affliction fell upon Mr. Webster this winter while at Washington. His daughter, Grace—his only daughter at that time—died, on the 23d of January, 1817. Her sickness and subsequent death, detained him from his seat in Congress during the month of January.

On the rising of Congress, Mr. Webster returned to Boston, and entered with diligence on the labors of his profession.

And these labors were both arduous and incessant; they were also lucrative. Clients crowded numerously upon him, bringing copious fees. He had not been two years in Boston, before his income from his professional practice was greater than that of any lawyer of his time, or any that had preceded him. His reputation grew with his means; and no one of his profession had before him such a brilliant and remunerating, if laborious, prospect.

CHAPTER III.

NOTWITHSTANDING the engrossing nature of Mr. Webster's professional pursuits, he found occasional time, "*vacare Musis*"—to gratify that love of reading and general acquisition, which has grown with his growth and strengthened with his strength. He also found time to comply with the earnest wishes of friends, who sought his contribution to the cause of history and literature. Belonging to such, is the Discourse he delivered at Plymouth, in December, 1820. It is not proposed to analyse this celebrated production here. Every one has read it who knows how to read, or what to read. But it may not be inopportune to introduce a remarkable prediction contained in it. Speaking of the energy, the enterprise and success of the natives of New England, the orator says: "It may be safely asserted, that there are now more than a million of people, descendants of New England ancestry, living free and happy, in regions, which hardly sixty years ago were tracts of unpenetrated forest. Nor do rivers, or mountains, or seas resist the progress of industry and enterprise. *Ere long, the sons of the Pilgrims will be on the shores of the Pacific.*"

It is but one of the many instances of far-reaching vision, amounting, indeed, to what the Scotch call *second-sight*, Mr. Webster has, on various occasions, exhibited. The comprehension of the Future from the study of the Past distinguishes, in truth, the man of intellect from the crowd: in ancient times it made the prophet; in modern, it forms the statesman.

Mr. Webster was not permitted to remain long undisturbed in the enjoyment of professional eminence and domestic comfort. Private friendship and State pride alike sought gratification in his return to the National councils. He had not been two years in his adopted State before he was urged, vehemently, by repeated application of friends to be a candidate for the House. On his refusal, an election to the Senate of the United States was offered him on the part of his friends in the Legislature. The present Chief Justice Shaw and late Judge Hubbard, both then distinguished members of the Legislature, called upon him at Dorchester, where he then was passing the summer, with this invitation. These various applications he entirely declined, seeking to devote himself exclusively to the practice of the Law. Attaining to the highest professional distinction, and emoluments, not only adequate to, but beyond his wants, he had enough for ambition, and could not look elsewhere safely for happiness. He followed his profession with a devotion that knew no interruption save from necessary relaxation. What time he could spare from the throng of clients, he resorted to field sports and rural exercise; nor did they profit less than himself from such occasional diversion. This, in truth, might be pronounced the most equable, and, perhaps, the most contented period of his life.

He was not insensible, however, to the calls of public duty. Besides serving a few weeks as member of the Legislature, he was an elector of President and Vice-President, at Mr. Munroe's second election in 1820, and also a delegate to the convention chosen to revise the Constitution of Massachusetts, in 1821.

In this convention he acted no unimportant part. In truth, it may be said, that there were few if any measures of much consequence adopted by it, which did not bear the impress of his mind. He encountered in this convention men of the Commonwealth, most eminent for their knowledge of the history and philosophy of legislation and jurisprudence, among whom it certainly cannot be invidious to mention the venerated name of JOHN ADAMS. This renowned patriot, sage, and statesman was drawing fatally near the close of life, but his last, as his earliest, thought was his country's. He had rocked the cradle of the Nation, and protected its infancy; and now that it had gained firmness of limb and muscular vigor, and could go alone, he still held over it an affectionate, and paternal care. Greatness and goodness attended upon him and ministered to his happiness. "Possessing," says Mr. Webster of him, "all his faculties to the end of his long life, with an unabated love of reading and contemplation, in the centre of interesting circles of friendship and affection, he was blessed in his retirement, with whatever of repose and felicity the condition of man allows."*

The Convention was indeed distinguished for the great array of intellect and public experience contained in it.

Mr. Webster took an active part in its proceedings, and made a number of energetic speeches in it; one upon a resolution relative to oaths of office; another upon a resolution to divide the State into districts, for the choice of Senators according to population; and a third upon the removal of judicial officers by the Governor and Council. These speeches, as their subjects would seem to require, were almost wholly argumentative. There was no need of rhetoric, and no oppor-

* In conversation once with Mr. Webster, he spoke to me of his last interview with Mr. Adams, which I give in as much as I recollect of his words: "I remember," he said, "the last time I ever saw Mr. Adams. It was the day I delivered the Discourse on the laying of the corner stone on Bunker Hill. I called to see him, to pay my respects to him, on my way home.

"It was a hot, sultry day in June. I found him lying on a sofa, apparently fatigued, and breathing not without difficulty. He had become fat, heavy, and unwieldy; his flesh hung down his face, full and flabby.

"He had an original nervous way of expressing himself, even in ordinary conversation. He always said something which you could afterwards recollect.

"While I was with him, and conversing on the common topics of the day, some one—a friend of his—came in and made particular enquiry of his health. 'I am not well,' he replied. 'I inhabit a weak, frail, decayed tenement; battered by the winds, and broken in upon by the storms; *and from all I can learn, the landlord does not intend to repair.*'"

tunity for the display of eloquence. On one occasion, however, Mr. Webster was provoked into something more impassioned and agitating than simple argument. It was in reply to a member, who had said that classifying towns for the choice of representatives, instead of giving every town a representative, however small its population, was forging chains and fetters for the people of Massachusetts. "Chains *and* fetters!" said Mr. Webster. "This convention of delegates, chosen by the people within this month, and going back to the people divested of all power within another month, yet occupying their space of time here in forging chains and fetters for themselves and their constituents! 'Chains *and* fetters!' A popular assembly, of four hundred men, combining to fabricate these manacles for the people—and nobody but the honorable member from Worcester with sagacity enough to detect the horrible conspiracy, or honesty enough to disclose it! 'Chains *and* fetters!' An assembly most variously composed—men of all professions and all parties—of different ages, habits, and associations—all freely and recently chosen by their towns and districts; yet this assembly in one short month contriving to fetter and enslave itself and its constituents! Sir, there are some things too extravagant for the ornament and decoration of oratory; some things too excessive even for the fictions of poetry; and I am persuaded that a little reflection would have persuaded the honorable member, that when he speaks of this assembly as committing outrages on the rights of the people, and as forging chains and fetters for their subjugation, he does as great injustice to his own character as a correct and manly debater, as he does to the motives and intelligence of this body."

These remarks, and especially the manner and countenance with which they were pronounced, somewhat excited the usually phlegmatic assembly ; many persons, then members, yet like to speak of the effect which they produced.

Mr. Webster's reputation daily augmenting as an orator and statesman, the desire on the part of his political friends to return him to Congress grew stronger and stronger ; till at length, in the fall of 1822, a Committee, consisting of Col. Thos. H. Perkins, Wm. Sturgis, Wm. Sullivan, John T. Apthorp and Daniel Messinger, called on him, with the information that he had been agreed upon as candidate for Representative to Congress. Col. Perkins read to him the vote by which he was nominated in the Convention, and the letter which was drawn up to accompany the vote ; and, saying that he had been instructed by the Convention to bring back no answer, retired with the rest of the Committee.

This severe and continued pressure finally overcame Mr. Webster's objections. He had declined with no Richard-like reluctance, eager to grasp what he seemed desirous to refuse, but from an honest, sincere, heart-felt reluctance. He knew, on entering public life again, he must abandon professional emoluments and domestic comfort. What honors he had already attained to in National Councils were sufficient to fill his ambition ; and he saw nothing in any prospect, however brilliant, of political life, to compensate for the sacrifice he needs must make to secure it.

Others would enjoy his labors. It seems the destiny of Genius to pursue unrequited toil, at least of that genius that labors in public affairs. There are services, too, that money cannot inspire nor compensate. The statesman may originate and digest a commercial code that gives competency and wealth to thousands—enhancing an hundred-fold the prosperity of his country. He may declare and conduct a necessary war, to secure its rights and extend its dominion ; or establish a permanent and honorable peace, with countless attendant blessings. He may open new marts for native industry, suggest new channels for enterprising labor, foster new inventions, and perfect new arts, in the plentitude of his power and capacity. Under him, a new spirit of enterprise may spring up ; new sources of wealth, hitherto unexplored, be revealed ; and all the great interests of society receive an impulse that can comprise no definition nor limit. But the prosperity of his country is his own martyrdom. For her greatness he sacrifices personal independence, domestic charities, health, and, too often, life itself. Pitt died at the age of forty-seven, overwhelmed with debt. He gave his country a position far above the powers of Europe and the world, and she gave him a funeral. Fox went down to the tomb, overtasked and worn-out, in mind and body. While the wounded sensibilities of Canning, excited almost to phrenzy by the proud man's contumely and the base man's ingratitude, could find no solace but in the grave.

Yet grateful England showers upon her well-deserving servants places, and pensions, and titles ; compensating, in the eyes of the unthinking multitude, perhaps, for broken health and shortened life. All England can do, at least she does with no niggard hand, but with a generosity becoming her history and greatness. All may not bring satisfaction to the bruised spirit, but it averts the charge of ingratitude from her.

In this country the statesman, who, by thought, word, or action, gains ascendancy for a policy or party, may add vast augmentation to the wealth of the country, and enable cool, plodding, enterprising individuals, by the accumulation of large fortunes, to obtain a seat in Congress, in the Cabinet, or even a Foreign Mission. But what does he gain for himself, for all his transcendant ability and service ? Injurious accusations, while living ; and in death, at best, a doubtful eulogy.

But Mr. Webster yielded to the importunate solicitations of friends, and was elected Representative to Congress from the city of Boston, in the fall of '22, by 1000 majority over Jesse Putnam.

Returning to the House, he found the Chair occupied, as he had left it, by Henry Clay. Other familiar faces he also met, and felt quite at home. Early in the session the question of the Greek Revolution was agitated ; and on the 8th of December, 1823, Mr. Webster presented the following resolution, in the House of Representatives : "Resolved, That provision ought to be made, by law, for defraying the expense incident to the appointment of an Agent or Commissioner to Greece, whenever the President shall deem it expedient to make such appointment." In introducing this resolution, Mr. Webster made an appropriate speech, in the beginning of which he said: "We must, indeed, fly beyond the civilized world; we must pass the dominion of law, and the boundaries of knowledge; we must, more especially, withdraw ourselves from this place, and the scenes and objects which here surround us, if we would separate ourselves entirely from all those memorials of herself which ancient Greece has transmitted for the admiration and the benefit of mankind. This free form of government, this popular assembly, the common council held for the common good, where have we contemplated its earliest models? This practice of free debate and public discussion, the contest of mind with mind, and that popular eloquence, which, if it were now here, on a subject like this, would move the stones of the Capitol,—whose was the language in which all these were first exhibited? Even the edifice in which we assemble, these proportioned columns, this ornamental architecture, all remind us that Greece has existed, and that we, like the rest of mankind, are greatly her debtors But I have not introduced this motion in the vain hope of discharging any of this accumulated debt of centuries. I have not acted upon the expectation that we, who have inherited this obligation from our ancestors, should now attempt to pay it to those who may seem to have inherited, from *their* ancestors, a right to receive payment. What I have to say of Greece concerns the modern, not the ancient; the living, and not the dead. It regards her, not as she exists in history, triumphant over time, and tyranny, and ignorance, but as she now is, contending, against fearful odds, for being, and for the common privilege of human nature."

In the course of his remarks he alluded in terms of severe, but just reprobation, to the character of the Treaty concluded at Paris in 1815, between Russia, Prussia, and Austria, commonly known under the title (assumed, one might suppose, in bitter mockery,) of "The Holy Alliance." Mr. Webster said, he wanted words to express his abhorrence of the abominable principles proclaimed in the preamble to this Alliance, the establishment of which was menaced by a million and a half of bayonets. "Human liberty may yet, perhaps," said he, "be obliged to repose its principal hopes on the intelligence and the vigor of the Saxon race. So far as depends on us, at least, I trust those hopes will not be disappointed."

To the question as to what this nation should do; whether we should declare war for the sake of Greece, and if not, if we would neither furnish armies nor navies, what we *should* do; what was in our power? he replied, in some of the happiest language even he ever commanded: "Sir, this reasoning mistakes the age. The time has been, indeed, when fleets, and armies, and subsidies were the principal reliances even in the best cause. But, happily for mankind, there has arrived a great change in this respect. Moral causes come into consideration, in proportion as the progress of knowledge is advanced; and *the public opinion* of the civilized world is rapidly gaining an ascendancy over mere brutal force. It may be silenced by military power, but it cannot be conquered. It is elastic, irrepressible, and invulnerable to the weapons of ordinary warfare. It is that impassable, inextinguishable enemy of mere violence and arbitrary rule, which, like Milton's angels,

> 'Vital in every part,
> Cannot, but by annihilating, die.'

Unless this be propitiated or satisfied, it is in vain for power to talk either of triumphs or repose. No matter what fields are desolated, what fortresses surrendered, what armies subdued, or what provinces overrun, there is an enemy that still exists to check the glory of these triumphs. It follows the conqueror back to the very scene of his ovations ; it calls upon him to take notice that the world, though silent, is yet indignant ; it shows him that the sceptre of his victory is a barren sceptre ; that it shall confer neither joy nor honor, but shall moulder to dry ashes in his grasp. In the midst of his exultation, it pierces his ear with the cry of injured justice ; it denounces against him the indignation of an enlightened and civilized age ; it turns to bitterness the cup of his rejoicing, and wounds him with the sting which belongs to the consciousness of having outraged the opinion of mankind."

President Monroe in his annual message to Congress, at the commencement of the session, had expressed a warm sympathy for the Greeks, in their struggle for independence ; and Mr. Webster's motive and action contemplated some reciprocation of his sentiments, on the part of the House, so far as it should approve them. His resolution was designed to have this effect, and no more. It failed, however, of favorable action. It took the House too much by surprise, accustomed rather to propositions of a temporary and local character.

Mr. Webster made one other great speech, during this Congress, upon a question of more domestic nature. It was upon the Tariff of 1824—which he opposed on the ground of expediency solely. The philosophic or economical character of this speech may be, in part, judged of from one quotation: "There is a broad and marked distinction," he said, "between entire prohibition, and reasonable encouragement. It is one thing by duties or taxes on foreign articles, to awaken a home competition in the production of the same articles; it is another thing to remove all competition by a total exclusion of the foreign article; and it is quite another thing still, by total prohibition, to raise at home manufactures not suited to the climate, the nature of the country, or the state of the population. These are substantial distinctions, and although it may not be easy in every case, to determine which of them applies to a given article, yet the distinctions themselves exist, and, in most cases, will be sufficiently clear to indicate the true course of policy."

Notwithstanding, however, the opposition of Mr. Webster, and the Massachusetts Representatives generally, the bill passed into a law, and New England was obliged to conform her temper and business to its operation.

In the fall of this year, 1824, Mr. Webster was re-elected to Congress, receiving 4,990 votes of the 5,000 thrown—an endorsement by popular favor probably without precedent in the annals of our political contests.

In the fall of this year, too, came off the election of President. ANDREW JACKSON, JOHN QUINCY ADAMS, WM. H. CRAWFORD and HENRY CLAY, were all candidates, and all received electoral votes for the Presidential office. The three first were returned to the House of Representatives, as being the three highest candidates; General Jackson, by an emphatic plurality of votes that indicated, beyond the entertainment of a doubt, his superior popularity. The potent influence, however, of Mr. Clay in the House was exerted in favor of Mr. Adams; and secured for him, in that body, a constitutional election. No intelligent man in the country believes that Mr. Adams' success was the consequence of any previous arrangement between himself and Mr. Clay, by which the latter, in such event, should become Secretary of State. Every candid man, on the contrary, will coincide in the opinion, expressed by Mr. Webster in relation to the subject, soon after the in-coming of the administration, in a speech at Fanueil Hall: "He would take this occasion to say, if his opinion could be of any value in such a case, that he thought nothing more unfounded than that that gentleman (Mr. Clay) owed his present position to any unworthy compromise or arrangement whatever. He owed it to his talent, to his prominent standing in the community, to his course of public service, not now a short one, and the high estimation in which he stands with that part of the country to which he belongs."

It is not to be denied, however, that many of Mr. Clay's friends regretted his acceptance of the highest office in Mr. Adams' administration,—because such acceptance involved the awkward necessity of an explanation. A *suspicion*, they thought, would attach to his motives, and always attend his position; and suspicion, they knew, often produced results as fatal to character as proven criminality. Like a reckless spendthrift, some held—he had secured a temporary gratification by the sacrifice of a certain, brilliant, and not distant, Future.

The question that most agitated the politics of the country during Mr. Adams' administration, was the PANAMA MISSION; a succinct historical account of which may not be impertinent here.

In the month of December, 1823, a formal invitation was addressed by Spain to the Courts of St. Petersburgh, Vienna, Berlin, and Paris, proposing to hold a conference at Paris, in order that the plenipotentiaries there convened, might assist Spain in adjusting the affairs of her revolted colonies in South America.

The proposed meeting, however, did not take place—perhaps in consequence of the decided course adopted by Mr. Canning on the part of England—who, in a conference with the French minister in London, declared distinctly and emphatically, that England would consider any foreign interference, whether by arms or intimidation, in the contest between Spain and her revolted colonies, as a conclusive reason for immediately recognising the independence of the latter.

It was under these circumstances, and at this crisis, that Mr. Monroe's justly celebrated declaration was made; that our government would consider any combination of European Powers to effect objects, whether of colonization or otherwise, in America, as affecting ourselves; that we should regard such combination as dangerous to ourselves, and should be prepared to meet it accordingly. This declaration had been agreed upon unanimously in Mr. Monroe's Cabinet after great deliberation, Mr. Calhoun and Mr. Crawford concurring in it with Mr. Adams. It met, too, with the entire concurrence of the country, as wise, seasonable, and patriotic. In England, also, it was received with no little enthusiasm. In the House of Commons, the leading minister expressed his full concurrence in the sentiments and opinions of the President, while his distinguished competitor in that body, of an opposite political party, declared that "no event had ever created greater joy, exultation, and gratitude, among the free men of Europe; that he felt a pride in being connected, by blood and language, with the people of the United States; that the policy disclosed by the message, became a great, a free, and an independent nation; and that he hoped his own country would be prevented by no mean pride or paltry jealousy, from following so noble and glorious an example."

"I look on the message of December, 1823," said Mr. Webster, in the House of Representatives, "as forming a bright page in our history. I will neither help to erase it, or tear it out; nor shall it be, by any act of mine, blurred or blotted. It does honor to the sagacity of the government, and I will not diminish that honor. It elevated the hopes, and gratified the patriotism of the people. Over those hopes I will not bring a mildew; nor will I put that gratified patriotism to shame."

The allies were deterred from taking any measures in concert with Spain for the subjugation of her colonies; but their menacing attitude for a time had alarmed the colonies themselves, and awakened the suspicions of our Government.

The Panama Mission seemed to be a corollary of President Monroe's message, to follow as a proper inference from the postulate, that American governments should have sole control of American interests. It proposed no belligerent measures; no departure from the neutral policy of the United States. It contemplated only a negotiation with the ministers of other American Republics, assembled in Congress at Panama, upon commercial and international relations. Whatever should be agreed upon in the Congress, was to be of no obligatory force whatever, or anywhere, unless afterwards duly ratified by their respective governments.

Mr. Webster, who had warmly approved the message of President Monroe, thought himself called upon to support a mission which seemed the legitimate result of its reasoning; and, in April, 1826, made an able speech upon the character and purposes of the mission.

It was unpopular, however, in the country; less, doubtless, from the nature of the objects it proposed to accomplish, than from the construction of the Administration which recommended it.

At the present day there is, probably, not a sentiment of the speech Mr. Webster made on the subject which would not meet the entire and hearty concurrence of four-fifths of the nation. The policy of Mr. Adams' Administration, in this respect, has outlived its general unpopularity.

It was in the summer of this year that Mr. Webster delivered his discourse in commemoration of the lives and services of John Adams and Thomas Jefferson. It would be in vain to look elsewhere for eulogies, expressed in more glowing and elevated language, or more appropriate to their subjects. The funeral orations of Bossuet, deservedly so celebrated, have not the repose, the dignity, nor sublimity of this. It sounds like a solemn anthem throughout. "Although no sculptured marble should rise to their memory, nor engraved stone bear record of their deeds, yet will their remembrance be as lasting as the land they honored. Marble columns may, indeed, moulder into dust, time may erase all impress from the crumbling stone, but their fame remains; for with AMERICAN LIBERTY ONLY can it perish. It was the last swelling peal of yonder choir, 'THEIR BODIES ARE BURIED IN PEACE, BUT THEIR NAME LIVETH EVERMORE.' I catch that solemn song, I echo that lofty strain of funeral triumph, 'THEIR NAME LIVETH EVERMORE.'"

The speech Mr. Webster has put into the mouth of John Adams in this funeral oration, as having been delivered by him in the Philadelphia Convention, in 1776, commencing, "Sink or swim, live or die, survive or perish, I give my hand and my heart to this vote," has been often mistaken for the production of Mr. Adams himself: it follows so inimitably Mr. Adams' style and forcible expression, Mr. Webster has been applied to, on several occasions, and by persons of literary pretensions, to know where and when Mr. Adams delivered the speech.

The address on laying the corner-stone of Bunker-Hill monument was made a year before, in 1825. It is too familiar to every one, to require even allusion to it.

In November, 1826, Mr. Webster was again re-elected to Congress, and by a vote of almost entire unanimity; but before he took his seat, under this canvass, he was chosen Senator of the United States, in place of the ever-lamented Elijah H. Mills, retired from ill health.*

The lives of literary characters or statesmen seem to be but, after all, an account of their productions and speeches. They appear to have no domestic life; or none, which is not absorbed in the engrossing nature of their pursuits. Mr. Webster's political life, however, has been varied by his professional

* According to the records, the vote of the Legislature stood thus: in the Senate, Daniel Webster had 26 votes; John Mills, 11; Edward Everett, 1; Levi Lincoln, 1. In the House, Daniel Webster had 202; John Mills, 82; scattering, 44.

avocations, and mitigated as before mentioned by his addiction to agricultural and rural occupations. In this latter respect, it has resembled Edmund Burke's, who was distinguished hardly less as an agriculturist than as a statesman and orator.

Mr. Webster had been obliged to relinquish a large portion of his practice—some of the most lucrative—by his re-entrance into public life. But in most important cases, he was still retained, particularly in such as were to receive final disposition in the Supreme Court of the United States. Of such, among others, was the famous case of *Gibbons* vs. *Ogden*, argued in the Supreme Court, in 1824, when the constitutional power of Congress to regulate commerce, *as a sole and exclusive power*, was insisted upon and triumphantly established by Mr. Webster—the judgment of the Court, as pronounced by Chief Justice Marshal, following closely the line of his argument. In this argument, he made use of the expression, *unit*, as applicable to the commerce of the United States, which General Jackson afterwards borrowed to describe the character of his Cabinet. Speaking of the relinquishment by States, of their former powers over commerce, to the general government, he said: "Henceforth, the commerce of the States was to be an *unit;* and the system by which it was to exist and be governed must necessarily be complete, entire, and uniform. Its character was to be described in the flag which waved over it, E PLURIBUS UNUM."

Other cases of moment Mr. Webster conducted in the

Supreme Court, which added to his reputation and income. It is not necessary to particularize them here.

Nor was Mr. Webster's public life unvaried by domestic calamities; which visit, without respect to persons, the families of the high as well as humble. The death of his daughter some years previous has already been alluded to: towards the close of this year, 1827, a still greater affliction fell upon him, in the loss of his wife. He was on his way to Washington, when she died. Her illness and subsequent decease prevented him from taking his seat in the Senate till January, '28.

In that august body, there were already men of national eminence. Besides Mr. Calhoun, who occupied the chair, and Mr. Forsyth, of Georgia, both of whom Mr. Webster had left the year before in the House, and with whom, in equal encounter he had measured swords, and Mr. Van Buren, more distinguished afterwards; there were Benton and Barton, of Missouri,—colleagues, but hostile, of great but opposite qualities—Woodbury and Bell, of New Hampshire, worthy Senators,—Tazewell and Tyler, of Virginia, ever in pursuit of abstractions, till they almost became such themselves,—Clayton of Delaware, Burnet of Ohio, and HAYNE, whose name needs no local designation. There were others, if not all of equal position in the country, all worthy of commemoration.

Mr. Webster's first encounter in the Senate was with Mr. Tazewell, upon the *Process Bill*, for regulating the proceedings of the United States Courts. The speeches were rather of a professional character, and there is little in them, or any incident connected with their delivery, to interest the general reader.

Mr. Webster exerted himself warmly in getting through a bill for the relief of the surviving officers of the Revolution; and, in April of this year, made an earnest and effective speech in its favor. Speaking of the conduct and services of the Revolutionary army, he said: "It had faithfully served and saved the country; and to that country it now referred, with unhesitating confidence, its claim and its complaints. It laid down its arms with alacrity; it mingled itself with the mass of the community; and it waited, till in better times, and under a new government, its services might be rewarded, and the promises made to it fulfilled. Sir, this example is worth more, far more, to the cause of civil liberty, than this bill will cost us. We can hardly recur to it too often, or dwell on it too much, for the honor of our country, and of its defenders. Meritorious service in civil war is worthy of peculiar consideration; not only because there is, in such war, usually less power to restrain irregularities, but because, also, they expose all prominent actors in them to different kinds of danger. It is rebellion, as well as war. Those who engage in it must look not only to the dangers of the field, but to confiscation also, and ignominious death. With no efficient and settled government, either to sustain or to control them, and with every sort of danger before them, it is great merit to have conducted with fidelity to the country, under every discouragement on the one hand, and with unconquerable bravery towards the common enemy on the other. So, sir, the officers and soldiers of the Revolutionary army did conduct."

Owing to the exertions of Mr. Webster, of Mr. Van Buren, and some other influential members, this bill of great remedial justice finally passed; his aid in the success of which, Mr Webster has said, on some occasion since, is one of the most grateful of his Congressional recollections.

At this session, a new Tariff bill passed: "the bill of abominations," as it was sometimes called. For the four years previous, New England had from mere necessity turned its attention to manufactures; and large investments had been made in that direction. There seemed to the people of that section no alternative, but to consider the cause and policy of the government as determined and fixed, and to govern themselves accordingly.

This new bill contained provisions, which seemed of a vindictive character; as if intended to punish such persons as had derived benefit from the Tariff of '24, though compelled to adopt it against their wishes.

"Sir," said Mr. Webster, in his speech on the passage of the bill—"I am sure there is nobody here, envious of the prosperity of New England, or who would wish to see it destroyed. But if there be such anywhere, I cannot cheer them by holding out the hope of a speedy accomplishment of their wishes. The prosperity of New England, like that of other parts of the country, may, doubtless, be affected injuriously by unwise or unjust laws. It may be impaired, especially, by an unsteady and shifting policy, which fosters particular objects to-day, and abandons them to-morrow. She may advance faster or slower; but the propelling principle, be assured, is in her; deep, fixed, and active. Her course is onward and forward. The great powers of free labor, of moral habits, of general education, of good institutions, of skill, enterprise, and perseverance are all working with her, and for her; and on the small surface, which her population covers, she is destined, I think, to exhibit striking results of the operation of these potent causes, in whatever constitutes the happiness, or belongs to the ornament of human society."

Notwithstanding the serious objections to the bill, Mr. Webster considered it his duty to vote for it, as the best alternative. Its defeat, he thought, would have a much more calamitous effect upon the interests of the country generally than its adoption.

He voted for it on the ground of expediency; and, it is upon that alone, his argument in favor of its passage rests. In vain should we look in this speech for that philosophical research, that entire mastery of the principles of political economy, and that intimate acquaintance with commercial and financial affairs which distinguished his speech against the Tariff of 1824. The present occasion, however, and the subject required less range of thought; action seemed rather demanded than argument; canvassing than eloquence.

Returning home at the end of the session, and meeting

some portion of his constituents in Faneuil Hall, Mr. Webster made allusion to the necessity under which he had found himself placed, by a most strange and unprecedented manner of legislation, of taking the evil of a public measure for the sake of its good. "The candid interpretation," said he, "which had been given to that vote, by those who disapproved it, and the assembling together here, for the purpose of this occasion, of those who felt pain, as well as those who felt pleasure, at the success of the measure for which the vote was given, afford ample proof, how far unsuspected uprightness of intention, and the exercise of an independent judgment, may be respected, even by those who differ from the results to which that exercise of judgment has arrived."

Another presidential canvass took place in the autumn of this year, the competitors in which were ANDREW JACKSON and JOHN QUINCY ADAMS. The popular voice, which had not invited Mr. Adams to the chair of state, precipitated him from it with emphatic utterance. On the 4th of March, 1829, General Jackson took possession of the vacated seat, with a temper not at all softened by the unnecessary delay of four years.

We approach now the most important era of Mr. Webster's intellectual life; in which he gained, at once and for ever, the highest rank as a debater and orator. No previous production of his, of whatever eminent ability, had prepared the minds of men for the display of such a vast variety of genius as he exhibited in this greatest intellectual contest of the age. He had always been equal to the occasion, it is true, but he had never hitherto encountered an occasion that demanded such infinite resources.

CHAPTER IV.

To understand fully the character and importance of the GREAT DEBATE, as it was called in the newspapers of the day, something should be known of the circumstances that immediately preceded and accompanied it, and of the more distinguished persons who participated in it.

It commenced, in the Senate of the United States, in the month of January, 1830, during the first session of the 21st Congress, and in the first year of the administration of Andrew Jackson; and lasted, with occasional but brief interruptions, four months.

Few persons ever attained to eminent position in this or any other country, under more auspicious circumstances, than Andrew Jackson. The idol of a party comprising much the larger portion of the constituency of the country, respected for the many liberal qualities of his head and heart, even by those who on conviction, or from interest, had opposed his elevation, this distinguished soldier in the earlier portion of his official career, gave assurance of an administration, equally brilliant and popular. In the presidential campaign of 1828, his competitor and immediate predecessor, JOHN QUINCY

ADAMS, whether from geographical position, or from a want of confidence among the masses in the policy of his measures, or purity of his intentions, or, more probable yet, from personal unpopularity, arising from a cold temperament and repulsive manners, had been signally and disgracefully defeated. No where, save in New England, and even there, perhaps, rather from local pride, than attachment to his person, or respect for his public character, had his canvass for re-election been honestly sustained. Elsewhere his efforts and those of his partisans had been vehemently rebuked. General Jackson received a majority in the electoral colleges unprecedented in the previous annals of party contention.

Undoubtedly one great reason of Mr Adams' unpopularity, was his cold, antipathetic manner, and the suspicion of selfishness it suggested, or at least aided greatly to confirm. None approached Mr. Adams but to recede. He never succeeded, he never tried to conciliate. He seemed one of those persons —not rare on earth—whose enjoyment stops in themselves; who find no pleasure in the indulgence of social feelings, and cherish no hope but of self-gratification. Friendship which receives and repays mutual benefits, which responds alike to good or adverse fortune, which removes us from entire isolation, expands the heart, lends new force to genius, and a nobler expression to thought, he never seemed capable of comprehending.

His mind, wonderfully precocious, was developed at the expense of his heart. Undue exercise of the one, as happens with the limbs of the body, dwarfed or weakened the other. He could elaborate vast schemes of political aggrandizement, construct stupendous tomes of incontrovertible logic, establish or demolish theories of perplexing ingenuity; but he was ignorant of an unselfish emotion, incapable of an ennobling expression, and constitutionally insensible to other than personal hopes and purposes.

All political dogmas, creeds and parties, were held by him in like consideration. He found them all equally fallacious and equally useful. He sacrificed no principle in espousing or repudiating either or all, for he had no principles to sacrifice. Without violence to his feelings or judgment, he admitted or rejected propositions and measures. He knew but one test of their soundness; how far they were useful, so far and so long they were right. In whatever other respect he resembled Cato Uticaensis, in one he differed from him materially. The *victa causa* never pleased *him*. The theory that failed was to him illogical; the party that fell, unprincipled.

This intense concentration of self upon self gave character to his countenance, manners, and habits. He seemed as cold, passionless and inscrutable as the Egyptian Sphynx, whose fate, too, his own resembled. He was successful while his secret was undiscovered, but that once exposed, he sunk for ever.

A disposition like his was its own Nemesis. Ever grasping at honors, success rather exasperated than satisfied him. While there was a step still higher, he was restless, discontented, morose, till he reached it; and when reached, the fear of its loss was greater than the pleasure of its enjoyment, and kept his mind in a constant turbulence. A want of sympathy for others, deadened his own sense of his elevation ; he knew not the increase of gratification from reflection. His merit, he thought, provoked service, which, like virtue, was its own reward. He therefore felt no gratitude, and acknowledged in his favors no distinction between friend and enemy. Success made him ungrateful, and defeat vindictive ; the one he easily forgot, the other he never forgave.

This harshness of character developed itself in his writings. Future ages no less than the present will suffer from its expression. A severe and unyielding logic pervades and oppresses all his productions. There is nothing to move the affections, to rouse the fancy, or open the heart, in any. In all the mighty volumes of lectures, essays, correspondence, state-papers and speeches with which he has terrified mankind, not a glorious sentiment, magnanimous idea, or soul-stirring expression occurs. They are all lava-like, destroying everything like fertilization.

Such a character could secure no permanent popularity. It was only to be appreciated, to be hated ; and the historian will be compelled to record, among the most prominent causes of Mr. Adams' ultimate defeat, his selfish, cold, unsympathetic heart, characterizing manner and action.

His successful competitor was cast in a different mould. Some virtues he had, and others he assumed. He was frank, affable, and impressionable ; and if not always sincere, always had the appearance of sincerity. It was easier to pardon his vices, than to acknowledge the virtues of his rival ; the arrogance of the latter offending self-love, more than the former the moral sense.

It is not to be denied, however, that he had one element of popularity which his opponent needed. This was his brilliant military reputation. His courage and conduct in several severe emergencies, and more particularly in one crisis of our public affairs, during the last war with Great Britain, had gained him the confidence and gratitude of his countrymen. This element of strength had been sensibly felt in the preceding canvass, and was perhaps the best solution of the almost incredible popularity which he enjoyed.

Still his military achievements, dazzling as they were, did not constitute his sole claim to popular favor. He had filled high stations in civil life, in National as well as in State Government ; in all of which he had given evidence of a determined will, an honest purpose, and sagacious judgment, that commanded the good-will of all classes. His character for moral, physical, and intellectual energy was known everywhere. He was thought to possess, too, qualities of mind rare in their independent excellence, and only less than miraculous in their combination. And hence there was a conviction, no more earnest than general, with the well-informed no less than with the vulgar, that he could cultivate with equal success the somewhat hostile arts of war and peace.

Everything, therefore, on his accession to power, seemed to

promise its safe and long continuance. The aspect of the political sky was unclouded. The almost unanimity of the popular vote by which this hero-statesman was borne into the Presidency, ridiculed the very idea of opposition. Hardly a latent inclination remained to combat the measures of his administration: the ability to do so with success seemed gone for ever.

Yet though the Administration had no cause of apprehension from outward assault, persons boasting more than ordinary sagacity foresaw, or professed to foresee, the inevitable cause of future and even early perplexity, to its councils. They discovered it in the character of the political alliance that obtained Gen. Jackson the Presidency; in the original formation of this alliance; its incongruous materials; its compulsory cohesion; and in the different ends proposed by its several constituent members.

It is to be admitted, that two divisions of the Democratic party, professing and advocating doctrines diametrically opposite, had leagued together to consummate, in the election of Gen. Jackson, their own political ascendancy—one contending for such a construction of the Constitution as authorized Congress to protect domestic manufactures, appropriate money for works of internal improvement, and, generally, to regulate and control all interests strictly national; the other, insisting upon a close, precise, narrow construction, which gave none but express powers, left nothing to inference or analogy. Of this latter division, the acknowledged head was Mr. Crawford, who had himself been a candidate for the Presidency in 1824, but in 1828 had withdrawn his former pretensions, and gone in, with all his friends, personal and political,—the most distinguished of whom was Mr. Van Buren,—in unqualified support of Gen. Jackson. This powerful and opportune accession had contributed in a great degree to the singularly rapid augmentation of the General's strength in the latter part of the canvass.

The division or section that urged a liberal construction of the Constitution, was at least as strong, from the position and ability of its leaders, and probably more so in the number of its rank and file. It had, beside, all the weight of precedent in its favor. It was a historical party. Its principles and policy had become firmly rooted in the public mind, from the countenance and furtherance they had met with from the two immediately preceding Administrations. Works of internal improvement, especially, had been recommended and carried out by the Administration of Mr. Monroe; and his policy in this respect, as in most others, had not only been warmly supported, but even extended by his immediate successor.

Between these conflicting opinions it was contended, Gen. Jackson would be compelled to decide; and it was predicted that his decision, which way soever it leaned, would necessarily disturb, if it did not completely destroy, the harmony of the party.

The necessity, however, for an election between these two principles had not yet arrived. Gen. Jackson was at this time sustained by a united, devoted and victorious party; and nothing had occurred thus far in his administration to diminish the attachment or weaken the confidence of the people, in his person and character.

On his accession, it seemed to be generally conceded that he would not be a candidate for re-election; and, in consequence, the party was about equally divided between the rival pretensions of Messrs. Calhoun and Van Buren. But however ardent the jealousy, and unremitting the watchfulness each of these eminent statesmen maintained towards the other, no open demonstration of hostility affected their own relations, or disturbed the intimacy of their mutual friends. Whatever there was of dislike, distrust, and growing alienation between them was studiously concealed, on either part, from the public. Their bearing towards each other seemed candid, even cordial; and from no outward indications could a suspicion of an approaching rupture be conjectured.

From the commencemeut of the administration up to the time of this debate, the most perfect understanding seemed to subsist between its distinguished chief, and the second officer of the Government, Mr. Calhoun. The latter had done the former some service, and was supposed at this time to have done him more. In the Presidential sweepstakes of 1824, he had postponed his own candidatecy, and had aided, by his personal and official influence, to secure for the General the nomination of Pennsylvania and its subsequent vote. In 1828, he had continued and redoubled his exertions. He also claimed, through his friends, to have defended, in Mr. Monroe's cabinet, Gen. Jackson's conduct in the Seminole war, and such at this time was the conviction of Gen. Jackson himself; who thus felt called upon from gratitude as well as from policy, to cultivate a close intimacy with the Vice President.

In consequence of this *entente cordiale*, Mr. Calhoun's partisans were appointed to some of the most lucrative and responsible positions in the Government. Mr. Ingham, one of the most devoted to his person and political fortunes, was placed at the head of the Treasury, the most influential office in the appointment of the President. While no persons were received at the White House with warmer cordiality than his nearest friends. Col. Hayne, of South Carolina, deservedly one of the most cherished of them, was a frequent attendant and particular favorite there. In truth, so strict and confidential an intimacy prevailed between the two highest officers of the Government at this time, that persons supposed to be in the possession of Gen. Jackson's confidence have not hesitated since to declare, that but for the quarrel Van Buren and Forsyth contrived soon after to get up between them, Gen. Jackson would have embraced the political principles and furthered the aspirations of the Vice President. Such indeed was then the common expectation. It was fated however that the same disturbing element, by means of which Harley and St. John ejected Godolphin and Marlborough from the councils and confidence of Queen Anne, should be, in the hands of men equally astute, the proximate cause of the rupture between Calhoun and Gen. Jackson. *Dux fœmina facti.*

Notwithstanding the immense majority of the suffrage, with which the administration had come into power, and the complete rout its opponents had sustained, it entertained towards the more prominent supporters of the late administration a mingled sentiment of vindictiveness and fear. There was nothing in its conduct towards them of the forbearance becoming a victorious and magnanimous party; on the contrary, their total annihilation seemed its dearest wish and only safe assurance of permanent establishment. The friends of the administration thought to pursue towards their chief opponents the same policy Tarquinius Superbus dictated to his son, who had gained possession by unworthy arts of an important city: to cut off the heads of the most noted men of the place, that there might be no rallying names for the multitude. Suppressing, therefore, for the time all inimical purposes towards each other, Calhoun-men and Van Buren-men, radicals and conservatives, nourished a common dislike, and united in acts of common hostility, against the chiefs of the late administration.

Their rancor and purpose were particularly directed against Mr. Webster, the acknowledged leader of the Anti-Jackson party in the Senate, whom they equally feared and hated. He had sustained the measures of the late administration with zeal, energy, and efficiency; had been its bulwark against all foes; and it had leaned upon him for support. During the recent canvass, too, he had been most active in Mr. Adams' cause; and by the warmth and vigor of his political action had controlled the nearly unanimous vote of New England against Gen. Jackson. The friends of the administration therefore could gratify, in his prostration, at once their animosity and their policy.

Contemporaneous authority gives encouragement to a suspicion that previous to the introduction of Foot's resolutions respecting the public lands, it had been determined by the leaders of the Jackson party to organize a crusade against Mr. Webster. The subsidized presses of the party were most violent in their abuse of his character, his history, and conduct. Mr. Adams and Mr. Clay having been driven into retirement, there remained, in the ranks of the opposition, no one but Mr. Webster of sufficient position, to embarrass to any great extent the new dynasty. To revolutionize New England, too, was a purpose they meditated and avowed; and, preparatory to its accomplishment, the overthrow of Mr. Webster seemed necessary.

Whether such a conspiracy was ever matured or not, one fact is incontestible; that the nearest and most powerful friends of both the Vice President and Secretary of State simultaneously attacked Mr. Webster, giving by the act to the world all the ordinary evidence of preconcerted purpose. Grundy and Livingston, Woodbury and Benton, Hayne, Rowan, and Forsyth, all participated in the onslaught.

It was a combination of great power, from the character and

position of the parties who composed it. They were all men of ability and reputation. Forsyth, it is true, took no open part in the discussion. He was none the less felt in the advice he gave, the information he afforded, and in the general direction of the strategy of debate. He was quick, cool, and of infinite resources.

Grundy and Livingston leave other reputation than what they achieved in this debate. It is fortunate for their fame it is so. For though the part they performed therein was not discreditable, nor even undistinguished, their names gained from it no additional lustre. They were no ordinary antagonists in a dialectic contest. Their talents were of a high order. Both had gone through an earnest intellectual training, which, with their natural capacity for affairs, made them alike admirable in speech or action. Grundy was, of all the Senate, nearest the President; and the moral prestige of this relation gave a direction, a weight, a conclusion to his words, not rashly to be overlooked. He was prudent of speech, and gave no offence, either by inconsiderate language or monotonous frequency, in his Parliamentary efforts. It is true, he was rather a debater than an orator, and more specious than profound. But he knew how to detect and expose the weak points of an adverse argument, and by the refutation of another's sophisms, divert attention from his own. There was an earnestness, withal, in his manner and countenance that invited attention and encouraged belief.

Livingston had a double claim to the respect of the Senate;

from the past as well as the present. In earlier days, he had been the representative—the sole representative—of the first commercial city in the Union, and was now a Senator from one of its most flourishing, though youngest States. In both capacities known and respected as an honorable man, intelligent and candid, polished in language and manner, and of unexceptionable character. He had seen a great diversity of character, of age, and institutions, and knew how to make his experience available, whether in the conduct of an argument, or in the establishment of a policy. Few Senators were held in greater esteem. He attacked no one; he indulged in no vituperative language. He opposed or defended measures, but he never questioned motives, nor calumniated persons. In his political career, while he never was guilty of a partisan meanness, he had on more than one occasion, displayed a liberality of opinion and conduct seldom recorded of politicians. He had advocated the Panama Mission, though opposed to the administration of Mr. Adams; an exhibition of moral courage that found few to praise and none to imitate it among his political associates. His reputation as a man of honorable bearing, cultivated intellect, and full experience in public life, preceding him to the Senate, gained him an influence there, which, from the day of his entrance, had daily increased.

Nothing but merit, and merit of the highest order, could have raised Mr. Woodbury to the positions he has occupied in the country. Successively, Judge of the Superior Court of his native State, Senator in Congress, Secretary of two Departments, and Judge of the Supreme Court of the United States; he has discharged the responsible duties of all these offices, if not with unequalled ability, most certainly with far more than ordinary capacity. He has better than realized the promise of his earlier days, and is in truth one of the rare examples of precocious talent confirmed and even strengthened in maturer age. But still he has not—he never had—the gift of eloquence. It is not his—it never was—to rouse, to agitate, to control the passions. Never on any one occasion of his various and eminent life, at the bar, the hustings, or senate-chamber, has he gained full mastery of the heart; ever prevailed upon his hearer to forget for one moment the speaker in his subject. His mind has rather a logical than imaginative character; has been more employed in analysing than creating. His sensibility has ever been subject to his reasoning faculties; and he has been compelled by the absoluteness of his mental organisation, to prefer serious argumentation, and unfertilising facts to fancy, taste, or eloquence.

Benton discharged all sorts of missiles at the head of an adversary, like a catapulta. Tropes, metaphors, similes, unsavory allusions, vituperative epithets, damnatory personalities, he hurled upon the victim of his temporary anger. He neither sought nor gave quarter; one of the regular Black Hussars of debate. His manner, if possible, was yet more excited than his language; and his voice more belligerent than either. His whole attitude was defiance, and each gesture a provocation. An indifferent auditor might suppose from the extravagance of his manner and language occasionally, that he was "running a muck." *Habet fœnum in cornu*, was at such times the proper solution of his conduct.

His speech was as often extraordinary, as his manner. He brought together such a mass of crude, undigested, indigestible compilations, overwhelming the subject-matter in its accidents, so much useless accumulation, disjointed and inconsequent facts, impertinent allusions, and loose though labored analogies, one could not but imagine that he had made a foray into the territory of history, and seized upon booty, of which he neither knew the value, nor cared for the destination.

Too often, whatever there was of invincible logic in his declamation, was lost in diffusive speech, in useless generalities, unconnected episodes, and uncalled-for personalities. His egotism at this time was almost ferocious ; it interpenetrated every part of his speech, and made it sometimes absurd, sometimes farcical, and always offensive. But whenever for a time he forgot himself in his subject, and became wholly absorbed in its consideration, he was an antagonist not to be despised. He had read much, he had observed much, he had hoarded much ; and all he had read, observed, or hoarded he held at a moment's command. If he could but bring his facts and illustrations into line, so as to bear down in compact array upon the enemy's centre, he pierced it and secured victory. But it was unfortunate for him that his facts, undisciplined and irregular, hung back upon the very point of engagement, and recoiled, like elephants in Indian armies, upon their own friends.

I speak of him as he was. Twenty years have passed since this debate took place. The closer study of mankind, of books, and himself, has liberalized his temper, chastened his style, and subdued his manner. He commits no such solecisms of thought or conduct as formerly. He arrogates less for his own position now, concedes more to his opponents'. His speech is less discursive and more argumentative; it neglects persons and embraces propositions; is more suggestive, logical, and final. Still, though his deportment has more suavity, his manner more amenity, and his speech less personality than of old, he does not roar you now as gently an 'twere any nightingale. He is Boanerges still.

On this occasion he headed the assault upon Mr. Webster, or, at least, upon New England. And it is not improbable that Mr. Webster had him in view, when in his second speech he spoke of "casting the characters of the drama, assigning to each his part: to one the attack, to another the cry of onset." A supposition the more likely, as Mr. Benton, in his speech, justified the suspicion that an onslaught upon New England and New England men, had been premeditated before the introduction of this debate.

Rowan had some knowledge of Constitutional law, and boasted more. His distinctions, however, were too nice, too refined, too sublimated for comprehension. It is doubtful if he understood his own propositions; it is certain none others could. His language was all esoteric: yet if he failed in convincing his audience, he succeeded in puzzling them; which was a half-victory, like the battle of Fontenoy. It is besides impossible to answer what it is impossible to understand ; so that, like the cuttle-fish, he often escaped detection in a darkness of his own creation.

His argument on this occasion was long and elaborate. *Sudavit et alsit*, to make it impregnable. It was mostly, however, tedious, illogical, inconsequent. Still there were fitful passages in it of indubitable merit, revealing some talent, and suggestive of more.

Hayne dashed into debate, like the Mameluke cavalry upon a charge. There was a gallant air about him, that could not but win admiration. He never provided for retreat ; he never imagined it. He had an invincible confidence in himself, which arose partly from constitutional temperament, partly from previous success. His was the Napoleonic warfare ; to strike at once for the capitol of the enemy, heedless of danger or cost to his own forces. Not doubting to overcome all odds, he feared none, however seemingly superior. Of great fluency and no little force of expression, his speech never halted, and seldom fatigued.

His oratory was graceful and persuasive. An impassioned manner, somewhat vehement at times, but rarely if ever extravagant ; a voice well-modulated and clear ; a distinct, though rapid enunciation ; a confident, but not often offensive address ; these, accompanying and illustrating language well selected, and periods well turned, made him a popular and effective speaker.

His *forte* was, still, rather declamation than argument: of close, severe ratiocination, which rejects everything but what leads to conviction, he knew but little. He had never mastered the science of dialectics; but he was not without a certain kind of specious logic, which, with the multitude of listeners, would pass for current coin. It had the form, the impress, and superficial appearance of the pure metal: but it wanted weight on examination, and had no genuine ring in its sound.

Col. Hayne was, incontestibly, the most formidable of Mr. Webster's opponents. He had more native and acquired ability than any of them. Such is the concurrent opinion of all who witnessed this great forensic contest; among others, of the Hon. Mr. Everett, of Massachusetts; who is himself no less distinguished as an orator, than for diplomatic ability and general acquirements. "It is unnecessary to state," says he, "except to those who have come forward quite recently, that Col. Hayne was a gentleman of ability very far above the average, a highly accomplished debater, an experienced politician, a person possessing the full confidence of his friends, and entirely familiar with the argument on which the theory controverted in Mr. Webster's speech rests."

The Senate was prepared to receive him favorably. He had been distinguished in the politics of his own State, and sanguine anticipations were indulged in by his friends of his great success when transferred to a larger sphere of action. Before his speeches in this great controversy, he had occasionally addressed the Senate, and displayed qualities of mind which seemed to justify all previous encomiums. He was, too, personally popular; an advantage of no inconsiderable nature in whatever contest or undertaking a man is engaged with his fellows. His consciousness of the favor with which everything he says or does is received, gives him a confidence and an energy which stimulate to great words or deeds.

Col. Hayne deserved his popularity. He had a courteous and frank address, conciliatory manners and deportment. He was high-minded and sincere; easy and agreeable in conversation; of great vivacity of intellect, and mercurial talent.

Such was the formidable character of the combination Mr. Webster found himself compelled by circumstances to meet. Never before, in Parliamentary annals, did one man encounter such fearful odds. The instance most like it, when Pulteney, and Pitt, and Littleton and Chesterfield, with others less distinguished, united in a simultaneous attack upon Walpole, differs in one important respect: Walpole had official position, the king's name, and a majority of the Commons in his favor—advantages that held him up even against intellectual superiority. Mr. Webster had nothing but himself to rely upon, with an equally powerful array against him. But both were intellectual combats, which, from the character of the actors and the various and momentous interests involved therein, have never been surpassed in any country or age.

To publish all the speeches of this great debate would require volumes. Still the debate itself would be hardly appreciated but from reference to the actors in it. The drama could not be complete, with even the subordinate parts left out: there was no such insignificant character in it but aided in some way the *denouement.*

The debate itself is a complete epic; only instead of wars and combatants, we have argument and orators. It is not a vulgar exhibition of brute strength—a gladiatorial or pugilistic encounter; but an intellectual struggle—the collison of mind with mind—the development of all the highest intelligence in man. The principles and truths evolved from its consideration will endure with the country for which they were intended, exalting its character and ennobling its destiny.

There were others of the Senate, less prominent before the public, of the dominant party, equally active in their exertions on this occasion: some of whom served as videttes, being thrown out in advance to gain and supply information respecting the enemy, and falling back upon the main body when battle joined. If the parts they performed were less distinguished than those of the persons enumerated, they seemed as necessary to success. Hardly a Senator of the dominant party but performed some duty on the occasion.

It is besides to be considered that the whole moral influence of the administration was directed against Mr. Webster. This, powerful at all times, was doubly so now. The iron will of Gen. Jackson subdued all minds to his: it penetrated and controlled every member of his administration or party, from the highest to the lowest. There is a species of fascination in a severe, inflexible will, that few have the moral energy to resist. It seems to partake of the character of destiny, in the certain accomplishment of its purpose. It paralyses weaker minds, and makes them the puppets of its action.

The one idea of Gen. Jackson's administration was devotion to himself. He allowed every variety of opinion and all freedom of conduct consistent with this. He forgave all moral obliquities with plenary absolution. There was with him but one unpardonable sin : it was resistance to his will.

He united in himself the whole force of his party. He was the Democratic party, as Louis XIV. was "the State." When he came into power, Democracy had local significations ; in one place it meant tariff, in another free trade ;—sometimes, "internal improvement," and sometimes, "strict construction." He gave it a definite name and character, which was not one in Georgia and another in Maine, but the same everywhere, of equal meaning and potency. The "Democratic" was lost in the Jackson party.

He gave it unity, consistency, and rigor of action. He could concentrate it upon one point, with one will. No one ever had round him more devoted followers—for though harsh to his enemies, he was always true to his friends. He would exert his whole power, outstrip all constitutional restrictions to gratify a friend. And this was the great secret of his power. His fidelity to friendship passed into proverb, and gained him the great heart of the nation.

What could not such a man at the head of such a party accomplish of good or evil? It is true, that so early in his administration, as the time now written of, he had not obtained the fearful ascendancy in the country or in Congress, as at a later period. But even now the influence of his character was deeply felt; and had he chosen to put forth his whole strength in any one direction, the result at least might long have remained doubtful.

But it is due the memory of this distinguished patriot, soldier, and statesman to say, that he never entertained towards Mr. Webster any of that vehemence of personal bitterness, which he sometimes exhibited towards his opponents. He was of too magnanimous character to hate a magnanimous foe. Mr. Webster never flattered, deceived, or abused him; never opposed his measures, but in an honorable manner, and with respectful language. In the campaign that had just terminated, Mr. Webster, in warmly supporting the cause of his rival, was careful to use no harsh language of him, or his pretensions: on the contrary, upon more than one occasion, when circumstances seemed to require the mention of his name, had spoken, in terms of fit encomium, of his distinguished military services. The General, who never forgot a favor or an injury, and who was as ready to acknowledge courtesy as to avenge insult, nursed, therefore, no feeling of personal unkindness for Mr. Webster; and the intercourse between these two eminent men at this time though not intimate nor cordial, was not unfriendly. Gen. Jackson tolerated, it may be, but did not second the attack upon Mr. Webster.

Still the Alliance used his name; which was "a tower of strength" to them. It whipped in the refractory, confirmed the wavering, and terrified the timid.

CHAPTER V.

On the 29th day of December, 1829, Mr. Foote of Conn. offered, in the Senate of the United States, the following resolution:

"*Resolved*, that the Committee on Public Lands be instructed to enquire into the expediency of limiting for a certain period the sales of the public lands to such lands only, as have been heretofore offered for sale, and are subject to entry at the minimum price. Also, whether the office of Surveyor General may not be abolished without detriment to the public interest."

Some skirmishing immediately occurred on the introduction of the resolution between Benton, Noble, Woodbury, Holmes, and Foote; but no one imagined it was soon to be followed by a regular engagement. A motion being made and carried to postpone the consideration of the resolution till the next Monday, the excitement for the time subsided.

When the resolution on the day specified came up for discussion, Mr. Foote remarked that in twelve years' experience in legislative assemblies, it was not within his recollection that a resolution merely for enquiry had been made a special order. As he could not discover any benefit which could possibly arise from introducing this practice, he should decline giving it his sanction, by taking the lead in the debate.

Some insignificant discussion hereupon having taken place among Senators, the resolution passed over for the day.

When it next came up for consideration on Monday the 18th, Mr. Benton took the floor and made a speech bearing evident indications of study and preparation. In the course of his remarks, he made a violent attack upon New England, its men and institutions. He denounced the policy of New England towards the West as illiberal and unjust—but extolled the generosity of the South. "The West must still look," he said, "to the solid phalanx of the South for succor."

The whole character of the speech revealed a previous intention to attack New England; and, in one he made subsequent to this, he asserted that he had been informed, during the vacation, of a design to introduce such a resolution, and declared his determination to meet it. It was brought in, he said, to forestall his own purpose. "It was introduced to check-mate my graduation bill! It was an offer of battle to the West! *I* accepted the offer; *I* am fighting the battle; some are crying out and hauling off; but *I* am standing to it, and mean to stand to it. I call upon the adversary to come on and lay on, and I tell him—

"Damned be he, that first cries hold, enough!"

This sentiment and the style of its utterance, are severely

Bentonian. A harmless resolution of inquiry respecting a measure of public policy was converted, in the alembic of his egotism, into a studied attack upon himself, or, it may be, he sought to make another seem the aggressor, in order to cover his own hostile intent.

He was followed by Col. Hayne, who, after returning his complimentary salute, "The South would always sympathize with the West," poured also a broadside into New England.

He placed in unpleasant contrast to the conduct of the South, the action of the Eastern States upon the question of the public lands, which he characterized as selfish and unprincipled. The East was unwilling—he said—that the public lands should be thrown open on easy terms to settlers, for fear of its being drained of population. It sought to retain its population at home for manufacturing purposes. "To create a manufactory of paupers, who should supply the manufactories of rich proprietors, and enable them to amass great wealth."

The suddenness of this attack upon New England, its warmth, and evident malice, took Mr. Webster by surprise. He could not but feel that the onslaught upon the East was intended as a personal attack. Yet he was conscious of having given no provocation to either of the aggressors. He had neither sought nor accepted an opportunity to annoy them.

He was not even aware of Mr. Foote's intention to introduce any such resolution; but yet he could see no harm in its terms or purpose, nor impropriety in its introduction. His relations with the two Senators, though not intimate, were not hostile. He had neither given nor taken offence. It has indeed been said, that at the close of the preceding session, Colonel Hayne had made a wanton and somewhat intemperate attack upon his opinions and conduct, which would have elicited a suitable reply, but for the interposition and entreaties of the Hon. John Reed and other members from Massachusetts, who feared a controversy between them at that time would endanger the satisfactory adjustment of some Massachusetts claim then on its passage though the Senate. Yielding to their solicitations, Mr. Webster discarded all resentful feeling and withheld a reply. To this, or some similar circumstance, he may be supposed to allude in the earlier part of his great speech, when speaking of Colonel Hayne's assault upon him. "Some passages, it is true, had occurred since our acquaintance in this body, which I could have wished might have been otherwise; but I had used philosophy and forgotten them." With Mr. Benton he had never been on terms of social or personal intimacy, yet bore towards him a relation of senatorial courtesy.

As soon as Colonel Hayne concluded his speech, Mr. Webster took the floor in reply. It was late, however, in the day, and he gave way on a motion from Mr. Benton to adjourn. In making the motion, Mr. Benton said he was unwilling that the harmony of the sounds which had just pervaded the Senate-chamber, and which still lingered upon the delighted tympanum of Senators, should be broken in upon by aught discordant.

The next day Mr. Webster replied to the speech of Colonel Hayne. The growing interest of the controversy attracted a more than usual crowd to the Senate. It appeared evident to every one, a drama of some importance was going on.

Mr. Webster defended the conduct of the Eastern States towards the West as regarded the question of the public lands, and disproved, by historical analysis, the accusation of neglect or hostility on their part. All that he said in this speech on the public lands, forms an admirable state paper. He had evidently carried the subject before in his mind. Alluding to the beneficial influence of the action of the general government upon the settlement of Ohio, and in the development of its vast natural resources, an action which he showed had been stimulated and directed by New England votes—he said, comparing the Ohio of 1794 with the Ohio of 1830: "And here, sir, at the epoch of 1794, let us pause and survey the scene. It is now thirty-five years since that scene actually existed. Let us, sir, look back and behold it. Over all that is now Ohio, there then stretched one vast wilderness, unbroken, except by two small spots of civilized culture, the one at Marietta, the other at Cincinnati. At these little openings, hardly a pin's point upon the map, the arm of the frontiersman had levelled the forest and let in the sun. These little patches of earth, themselves almost shadowed by the overhanging boughs of that wilderness, which had stood and perpetuated itself, from century to century, ever since the Creation, were all that had been rendered verdant by the hand of man. In an extent of hundreds and thousands of square miles, no other surface of smiling green attested the presence of civilization. The hunter's path crossed mighty rivers, flowing in solitary grandeur, whose sources lay in remote and unknown regions of the wilderness. It struck upon the North, on a vast inland sea, over which the wintry tempests raged as on the ocean; all around was bare creation. It was a fresh, untouched, unbounded, magnificent wilderness! And, sir, what is it now? Is it imagination only, or can it possibly be fact, that presents such a change as surprises and astonishes us, when we turn our eyes to what Ohio now is? Is it reality or a dream, that in so short a period as even thirty-five years, there has sprung up on the same surface an independent State, with a million of people? A million of inhabitants! An amount of population greater than all the Cantons of Switzerland; equal to one-third of all the people of the United States when they undertook to accomplish their independence. If, sir, we may judge of measures by their results, what lessons do these facts read us upon the policy of the government? what inferences do they not authorise upon the general question of kindness or unkindness? what convictions do they enforce, as to the wisdom and ability, on the one hand, or the folly and incapacity on the other, of our general management of Western affairs? For my own part, while I am struck with wonder at the success, I also look with admiration at the wisdom and foresight which originally arranged and prescribed the system for the settlement of the public domain."

In relation to the comparative aid afforded by the East and South to the settlement of the West, Mr. Webster said: "I undertake to say, sir, that if you look to the votes on any one of these measures, and strike out from the list of ayes the names of New England members, it will be found that in every case the South would then have voted down the West, and the measure would have failed."

In conclusion Mr. Webster said: "The Senate will bear me witness that I am not accustomed to allude to local opinions, nor to compare nor contrast different portions of the country. I have often suffered things to pass which I might properly enough have considered as deserving a remark, without any observation. But I have felt it my duty on this occasion, to vindicate the State which I represent from charges and imputations on her public character and conduct, which I know to be undeserved and unfounded. If advanced elsewhere, they might be passed, perhaps, without notice. But whatever is said here is supposed to be entitled to public regard, and to deserve public attention; it derives importance and dignity from the place where it is uttered. As a true representative of the State which has sent me here, it is my duty, and a duty which I shall fulfil, to place her history and her conduct, her honor and her character, in their just and proper light.

"While I stand here as representative of Massachusetts, I

will be her true representative, and by the blessing of God, I will vindicate her character, motives, and history, from every imputation, coming from a respectable source."

If Mr. Webster betrayed in this speech an unusual warmth of manner and language, his sufficient apology is the provocation he had received. New England,—and more particularly Massachusetts, his foster-mother,—had been gratuitously assailed, and, as he could not but believe, with direct reference to himself. He had been struck at where his sensibilities were deepest and keenest—in his love of home ;—and had he remained silent or even contented himself with simply repelling the attack, his constituency and the world would have pronounced him craven. This was not besides the sole provocation he had received ; this was not the solitary occasion on which his temper had been sorely tried. The dominant party in the Senate, mad with its excessive victory, had previously teazed and goaded him. He had borne much,—some thought too much,—with "a patient shrug." The time had come when, in more than his own opinion, he should take the field in earnest.

On Tuesday, January 21st,—the day after Mr. Webster's speech,—the Senate resumed again the consideration of Mr. Foote's resolution.

Before the debate recommenced, Mr. Chambers, of Md., rose and expressed a hope that the Senate would consent to postpone further consideration of the resolution till the Monday following, as Mr. Webster who had taken part in it and wished to be present at its continued discussion had unavoidable engagements elsewhere.

There was a case of some importance on argument before the Supreme Court in which Mr. Webster was retained as counsel. Compelled to watch its progress, for he knew not at what moment he might be called upon to address the Bench, he had not been able to command more than an occasional presence in the Senate. He was not present when the resolution was introduced, nor more than a fractional portion of the time while Mr. Benton spoke.

The request was denied him. Col. Hayne rose in evident agitation, and insisted that the debate should go on without postponement. He said with some superciliousness of manner and with an angry intonation of voice, that he saw the gentleman from Massachusetts in his seat; and presumed, if he really desired it, he could make an arrangement which would enable him to be present at the discussion that day. He would not consent that the subject should be postponed, until he had had an opportunity of replying to some of the observations which had fallen from the gentleman the day before. Putting his hand to his heart, he said, "he had something there, which he wished to get rid of. The gentleman had discharged his fire in the face of the Senate; and he demanded an opportunity of returning the shot."

"Then it was"—to use the words of a distinguished member of Congress from a Southern State who was present on the occasion—"that Mr. Webster's person seemed to become taller and larger. His chest expanded, and his eyeballs dilated. Folding his arms in a composed, firm, and most expressive manner, he exclaimed: 'Let the discussion proceed. I am ready. I am ready *now* to receive the gentleman's fire.' Oh, my dear sir, I wish I could convey to you even some faint idea of the true grandeur that then marked his manner and countenance."

Mr. Benton, who had gained the floor the day previous on the conclusion of Mr. Webster's remarks, then rose and addressed the Senate for an hour. In the earlier part of the speech, he undertook to remove all pretension of Nathan Dane to the authorship of the Ordinance of '87, which he claimed for Thomas Jefferson. Speaking as if he had accomplished the undertaking, beyond the possibility of denial, he said: "But yesterday the name of Nathan Dane, of Beverly, Massachusetts, hung in equipoise against half the names of the sages of Greece and Rome. Poetry and eloquence were at work to blazon his fame ; marble and brass, and history and song, were waiting to perform their office. The celestial honors of the apotheosis seemed to be only deferred for the melancholy event of the sepulchre. To-day, all this superstructure of honors, human and divine, disappears from the earth. The foundation of the edifice is sapped ; and the superhuman glories of him, who, twenty-four hours ago, was taking his station among the demi-gods of antiquity, have dispersed and dissipated into thin air—vanishing like the baseless fabric of a vision, which leaves not a wreck behind."

Apart from the egotism, somewhat atrocious of the speech, there was a good deal of merit in it. It displayed no little ingenuity of argument, and much power of invective, with some considerable amount of political and miscellaneous learning; the latter all poured out, however, in one turbid gush.

The debate had by this time assumed a character that left no doubt of the intention of its promoters. To disinterested persons who had been thus far present in the discussion, nothing seemed now more evident than a determined purpose on the part of the majority to crush Mr. Webster. Out of the Senate, his approaching and inevitable discomfiture was among the friends of the Administration the prominent and most agreeable topic of conversation; in their opinion his doom was certain; for he was not only to be assailed by the ordinary force of the party, but was fated to encounter the irresistible attack of the great statesman and orator, Gen. HAYNE, of South Carolina—the very Achilles of the South; unlike Homer's hero, however, *vulnerable nowhere!* Benton complained in the open Senate that there would be nothing left for him to do; while Rowan and those near him congratulated themselves that they too at least would be "in at the death."

The warm blood of Col. Hayne could not brook the postponement of vengeance. He besought his friend from Missouri to yield the floor, while he replied to the Senator from Massachusetts. Mr. Benton gave a cheerful assent; but before Col. Hayne commenced, Mr. Bell, of New Hampshire, made another motion to adjourn till the Monday following. This motion was lost by a strict party vote.

Col. Hayne then rose and entered upon his speech. His exordium was respectable in point of ability, and gave assurance of a well-prepared speech. Every one must judge of it for himself. The high estimate that had previously been formed of his talents and character disposed the Senate and audience to listen attentively; and there was much in the earlier part of the speech particularly to confirm the common opinion of his abilities and to command attention.

As he proceeded, his tone and language became more vehement: his allusions more personal. There was an angry inflection in his voice, indicative of loss of temper. His bearing betrayed a good deal of self-confidence, at times almost arrogance. He seemed certain of victory, and only doubtful how much of his strength he should put forth. Violent as were his personalities, and bitter his invective, they were less intolerable yet than the insolence of his charity; for he seemed to arrest ever and anon "the thunder in mid volley," not to annihilate all at once his inevitable victim.

Sympathizing and exulting friends surrounded him, from whose countenances he read the apparent success of his philippic. They urged him on with looks and encouraging words. The eye of the Vice-President, which, alone of his features, ever indicated an emotion, shone approvingly. Nor did he confine his assistance to a glance of approbation. Constantly during the progress of the discussion, he sent notes, suggestive, illustrative and advisatory to the orator, by one of the pages of the Senate.

Col. Hayne had other advisers and other contributors in and out of the Senate, who supplied him with all the damnatory paragraphs the press had ever thrown out, in its moments of greatest excitement against New England, Mr. Webster, or his friends. They lie piled upon the orator's desk—Pelion upon Ossa—"an ass's load."

In speaking afterwards of such attempts to injure him, Mr. Webster said: "The journals were all pored over, and the reports ransacked, and scraps of paragraphs and half sentences were collected, put together in the falsest manner, and then made to flare out as if there had been some discovery. But all this failed. The next resort was to supposed correspondence. My letters were sought for, to learn, if, in the confidence of private friendship, I had never said anything which an enemy could make use of. With this view, the vicinity of my former residence was searched, as with a lighted candle. New Hampshire was explored from the mouth of the Merrimack to the White Hills."

Who of Mr. Webster's political opponents in or out of the Senate acted as "scavengers" on this occasion, it were unnecessary, if it were possible, to mention. They were fully punished in the failure of their unmanly efforts. The greatest, perhaps the only punishment, the unprincipled machinator feels, is a sense of useless rascality.

Col. Hayne spoke this day, Thursday, January 21st, a little

more than an hour. The Senate then adjourned over till Monday following. To give the Senator from Massachusetts fair warning of the fate that awaited him, Col. Hayne, on the conclusion of this day's remarks, spoke as follows: "Sir, the gentleman from Massachusetts has thought proper for purposes best known to himself, to strike the South through me; the most unworthy of her servants. He has crossed the border, he has invaded the State of South Carolina, is making war upon her citizens, and endeavoring to overthrow her principles and her institutions. Sir, when the gentleman provokes me to such a conflict, I meet him at the threshold—I will struggle, while I have life, for our altars and our firesides, and if God gives me strength, I will drive back the invader discomfited. Nor shall I stop there. If the gentleman provokes war, he shall have war. Sir, I will not stop at the border; I will carry the war into the enemy's territory, and not consent to lay down my arms, until I shall have obtained 'indemnity for the past, and security for the future.' It is with unfeigned reluctance that I enter upon the performance of this part of my duty: I shrink, almost instinctively, from a course, however necessary, which may have a tendency to excite sectional feelings, and sectional jealousies. But, sir, the task has been forced upon me, and I proceed right onward to the performance of my duty; be the consequences what they may, the responsibility is with those who have imposed upon me the necessity. The Senator from Massachusetts has thought proper to cast the first stone, and if he shall find, according to a homely adage, that 'he lives in a glass-house,' on his head be the consequences."

This language is minatory: it is also somewhat arrogant. As if the consummation necessarily followed the menace. The Senator from South Carolina spoke *ex cathedrâ*. He was buoyed up by the applause of friends and his own sanguine temperament.

The Senate adjourned over to the following Monday. The town was full of excitement. The severe nature of Col. Hayne's attack, the ability with which it was conducted, his great reputation, the eminence of the combatants, and the doubtful issue of the contest afforded ample scope for various discussion. The friends of Col. Hayne were much elated at what they considered his brilliant *debut*, and confidently predicted his ultimate triumph. Mr. Webster's friends doubted, and hoped.

A simultaneous and seemingly preconcerted attack upon New England from the leaders of Southern and Western Democracy raised among the Eastern men, of whatever political opinions, a common feeling. Party-spirit was wholly merged in wounded national (or local) pride. Sympathy for the cause, and for Mr. Webster in the isolated position he held against such a powerful array, overrode for the time all prejudice against his person or political principles. The Yankee predominated over the Democrat.

When the Senate convened again on Monday, the agitation in men's minds, growing daily stronger from the previous adjournment, had gained a feverish character. The long time afforded Col. Hayne for additional preparation, his rumored consultations with the Vice-President, and the confident manner both of himself and friends added new force to the excitement, and promised richer entertainment from the discussion: so the Senate-chamber was more filled and earlier than usual.

Col. Hayne commenced this day with a history of the Hartford Convention, illustrated by the documentary evidence his "scavengers" had hunted up. The whole affair is a tedious farrago, which not even his name could elevate into importance. Four columns and a half of the Intelligencer were crowded with such matter—quotations from newspapers, pamphlets and sermons—read to the Senate "with good accent and good discretion." His elocution was fluent and melodious; this alone reconciled Senate and audience to what would in itself have been absurdly tedious.

Passages will be found in the speech of real eloquence, sparsely scattered, however. There is no sustained power throughout, but acting only at fitful intervals. The best hit perhaps the speaker made was his charge against Mr. Webster of inconsistency upon the subject of the Tariff. It is conveyed, too, in language better selected and more expressive than his usual style. Speaking of Mr. Webster's anti-tariff speech in '24, Col. Hayne said: "On that occasion he, the gentlemen, assumed a position which commanded the respect and admiration of his country. He stood forth the powerful and fearless champion of free-trade. He met in that conflict the advocates of restriction and monopoly, and they 'fled from before his face.' With a profound sagacity, a fulness of knowledge, and a richness of illustration that has never been surpassed, he maintained and established the principles of commercial freedom on a foundation never to be shaken. Great indeed was the victory achieved by the gentleman on that occasion; most striking the contrast between the clear, forcible and convincing arguments by which he carried away the understanding of his hearers, and the narrow views and wretched sophistry of another distinguished orator, who may be truly said to have 'held up his farthing candle to the sun.' Sir, the Senator from Massachusetts on that (the proudest day of his life) like a mighty giant, bore away upon his shoulders the pillars of the temple of error and delusion, escaping himself unhurt, and leaving his adversaries overwhelmed in its ruins. Then it was that he erected to free-trade a beautiful and enduring monument, and 'inscribed the marble with his name.'"

The vehemence of the orator's language and the earnestness of his manner, produced no little effect upon his audience. They naturally begat sympathy. No one had time to deliberate upon his words, or canvass his statements. The dashing nature of the attack; the assurance, almost insolence, of its tone; the severity and apparent truth of the accusations, confounded almost every hearer. The immediate impression from the speech was most assuredly disheartening to the cause Mr. Webster upheld. The friends of the Administration qualified by no regard for person or place the extent of their exultation. Congratulations from almost every quarter were showered upon the speaker. Mr. Benton said, in the full Senate, that much as Col. Hayne had done before to establish his reputation as an orator, a statesman, a patriot, and a gallant son of the South, the efforts of that day would eclipse and surpass the whole. It would be an era in his senatorial career which his friends and his country would mark and remember, and look back upon with pride and exultation.

Nor was lavish praise of the speech confined to Mr. Benton or the Senate. Abroad, it gained equal commendation. The press of the Administration extolled it as the greatest effort of the time, or of other times. Chatham, nor Burke, nor Fox, had surpassed it, in their palmiest days. Immense exertions were made to throw it into general circulation, that public opinion might be forestalled in regard to the great question of the constitutional power of the General Government.

Satisfaction, however, with the speech even among the friends of the orator was not unanimous. Among others, Mr. Calhoun, and Mr. Iredell, a Senator from North Carolina, doubted. These gentlemen knew, for they had felt Mr. Webster's power. They knew the great resources of his mind; the immense range of his intellect; the fertility of his imagination; his copious and fatal logic; the scathing severity of his sarcasm, and his full and electrifying eloquence. To a friend of Hayne's, who was praising the speech, Mr. Iredell said: "He has started the lion—but wait till we hear his roar, or feel his claws."

Gloomy fears, in the meantime, for the most part, oppressed Mr. Webster's friends. The savageness of the attack, its seeming premeditation and powerful support gave them no encouragement of a successful resistance. They felt for Mr. Webster; they also felt for themselves. Their local pride, their love of fame, the first to spring up in the heart of man, the last to leave it, was deeply mortified.

Everywhere during the evening and night following, the merits of the speech were canvassed. The town was divided into geographical opinions. One's home could be distinguished from his countenance, or manner; a Southerner's by his buoyant, joyous expression, and confident air; a Yankee's, by his timid, anxious eye, and depressed bearing. One walked with a bold, determined step, that courted observation; the other, with a hesitating, shuffling gait, that seemed to long for some dark corner, some place to hear and see, and be unseen.

Immediately upon the conclusion of Colonel Hayne's speech, Mr. Webster took the floor in reply; but, it being near four o'clock in the afternoon, gave way to a motion for adjournment. Mr. Everett has kindly furnished the writer with some notes of a conversation he had with Mr. Webster the evening before his speech.

"Mr. Webster conversed with me freely and at length upon the subject of the reply, which he felt it necessary to make to Colonel Hayne's speech. He regarded that speech as an entirely unprovoked attack upon the Eastern States, which it was scarcely possible for him, as a New England Senator, to leave unnoticed. He thought Colonel Hayne's speech, however, much more important in another point of view, that is as an exposition of a system of politics, which, in Mr. W.'s opinion, went far to change the form of government from that which was established by the Constitution, into that (if it could be called a government) which existed under the confederation. He expressed his intention of putting that theory to rest for ever, as far as it could be done by an argument in the Senate Chamber.

* * * * * * * * *

"I never saw him more calm and self-possessed, nor in better spirits; and in fact the dry business tone in which he partly talked and partly read over his points to me, gave me some uneasiness, for fear he was not sufficiently aware how much was expected of him the next day."

An anecdote of Mr. Webster's equanimity under the infliction of Hayne is told by another friend, who called on Mr. Webster the same evening. While he was present, Mr. Webster laid down on the sofa for a nap—"his custom sometimes of an afternoon"—and after a while was overheard laughing to himself. On being questioned as to what amused him so, he replied: "I have been thinking of what Col. Hayne said today about Banquo's ghost; and I am going to get up and make a note of it."

Col. Hayne, it will be remembered, had in his second

speech accused Mr. Webster of sleeping upon his first. ' The mere matter of fact," said Mr. W. in his reply, ' is undoubtedly true. I did sleep on the gentleman's speech and slept soundly; and I slept equally well on his speech of yesterday to which I am now replying." In truth, Col. Hayne's attack, furious as it was, had cost him neither loss of appetite, temper or sleep."

It is not to be disguised, however, that his friends,—even his most intimate,—entertained fearful apprehensions. Mr. Webster's adversaries had selected their own time for attack, and made every preparation they thought necessary to ensure success. They were confident in their numbers, confident from their position and individual importance, and confident in the strength of their cause. There is always something, too, of advantage in assuming the aggressive; courage suggests, and virtuous anticipations await an attack: while a defensive position is seemingly an acknowledgment of weakness.

The momentous interests involved in the discussion staggered the minds of many. The pernicious heresy of nullification, tolerated if not encouraged in the high places of the Administration, threatened the constitution and the union of the States. It had already gained in different sections of the country too great a prevalence; and if now successfully advocated in the Senate of the United States, little hope could be entertained of safety or of more than brief duration for our national institutions.

The friends, therefore, of the Union, no less than Mr. Webster's personal friends, could not but feel the deepest solicitude in the result of the controversy; a solicitude amounting at times almost to despondency. They could hardly believe that it was in the power of one man, no matter how great his endowments, to roll back the strong current that seemed likely to overwhelm the ancient landmarks. All portents looked gloomy, they thought; darkness and danger were everywhere around them, and they saw no means of emerging from their great peril but with great loss and discomfiture.

The night, therefore, came down gloomily and heavily upon them. They had no pastimes and little sleep that night, and rose in the early morning, unrefreshed and anxious; determined, however, with one mind, to resort in good season to the Capitol.

CHAPTER VI.

When Cineas returned from his mission to Rome, he was asked by his master Pyrrhus, how the Roman Senate appeared. "Like an assembly of kings," he replied.

The Senate of the United States twenty years ago may not have presented the grave and majestic character of the Roman Senate. Our Senators wore not the flowing robes, nor still more flowing beards of the Conscript Fathers. But it was composed of men who could have understood Cicero as well as the audience he addressed, and replied to him better; of men, too, not inferior, in physical organization, or intellectual expression, to any Senate Rome ever boasted.

Where, among the most Patrician blood of Rome, could have been found more intellectual majesty than in the countenances of Webster and Calhoun, more dignity than in their bearing, more honor than in their character, or more grandeur than in their eloquence? In whatever assembly placed, they would have given to it unrivalled distinction.

Nor were they the sole persons of eminent ability, or distinguished mien, in the Senate. There were others only less remarkable for both. The thoughtful eye and expansive brow of Woodbury, the refined, gentlemanly, and expressive countenance of Forsyth, the gallant air and intellectual features of Hayne, the somewhat supercilious but determined bearing of Benton, the tall form and marked expression of Bell, the well-defined and rather majestic lineaments of Clayton—these characteristics, with those of other Senators no less distinguished, could not fail to convey to the spectator the impression of great intellectual and moral superiority. It was an assembly to be a member of which might have satisfied the most high-reaching ambition. It was an assembly the aggregate ability of which, for the number of its members, has probably never been surpassed, if equalled, in any representative body of the world.

The very character of the Senate made its members more eager to distinguish themselves in it. "Alexander fights when he has kings for his competitors." Rivalry, always natural to the heart, became more emulous, more earnest, more intense, with such a field for its encouragement and exhibition; when men were judges of the intellectual strife, who could themselves have taken an equal part in it, had occasion demanded.

It was not alone the combined strength of the administration party in the Senate Mr. Webster had to fear. He could not but be in doubt respecting his political allies. The character of the minority at this time was somewhat anomalous. It was composed of Federalists of the old school, who had adhered to the younger Adams, notwithstanding his gross tergiversations; of those Republicans, who, in the preceding canvass, from personal or local rather than from political considerations, had preferred Mr. Adams to his competitor; and of "National Republicans" so called—a party formed indifferently of the two others. To make an argument which should satisfy all without offending either of these classes seemed a task difficult to be accomplished.

Fortunately for the country and his own fame, his doubts, on the subject, were removed. His warmest friends urged with great eagerness upon him an unequivocal, unreserved declaration of his views. None were more trusted, nor esteemed by him, than SAMUEL BELL, then a Senator from New Hampshire. Originally a Federalist, he had gone over to the Republican party, early on the accession of Jefferson, and had supported his administration zealously and efficiently. He had advocated and defended the war with Great Britain, and all other measures of the Republican party up to the Presidential canvass of 1824. On that occasion, as well as four years later, without any violence, as he supposed, to his political principles or antecedents, he had favored the pretensions of Mr. Adams. From his history, character, and general knowledge of persons and measures, he was perhaps the best exponent of the intentions and sentiments of the somewhat mottled party, opposed to the administration of General Jackson.

So at least Mr. Webster thought; and on the morning of

the speech, after he had gone to the Capitol, he called Mr. Bell into the robing-room of the Senate, and told him his difficulty. "You know, Mr. Bell," said he, "my constitutional opinions. There are, among my friends in the Senate, some who may not concur in them. What is expedient to be done?" Mr. Bell, with great emphasis of manner, advised him to speak out, boldly and fully, his thoughts upon the subject. "It is a critical moment," said he, "and it is time, it is high time the people of this country should know what this Constitution *is*." "Then," replied Mr. Webster, "by the blessing of heaven, they shall learn, this day, before the sun goes down, what I understand it to be."

It was on Tuesday, January the 26th, 1830,—a day to be hereafter forever memorable in Senatorial annals,—that the Senate resumed the consideration of Foote's Resolution. There never was before, in the city, an occasion of so much excitement. To witness this great intellectual contest, multitudes of strangers had for two or three days previous been rushing into the city, and the hotels overflowed. As early as 9 o'clock of this morning, crowds poured into the Capitol, in hot haste; at 12 o'clock, the hour of meeting, the Senate-Chamber,—its galleries, floor and even lobbies,—was filled to its utmost capacity. The very stairways were dark with men, who hung on to one another, like bees in a swarm.

The House of Representatives was early deserted. An adjournment would have hardly made it emptier. The Speaker, it is true, retained his chair, but no business of moment was, or could be, attended to. Members all rushed in to hear Mr. Webster, and no call of the House or other Parliamentary proceedings could compel them back. The floor of the Senate was so densely crowded, that persons once in could not get out, nor change their position; in the rear of the Vice-Presidential chair, the crowd was particularly intense. Dixon H. Lewis, then a Representative from Alabama, became wedged in here. From his enormous size, it was impossible for him to move without displacing a vast portion of the multitude. Unfortunately too, for him, he was jammed in directly behind the chair of the Vice-President, where he could not see, and hardly hear, the speaker. By slow and laborious effort—pausing occasionally to breathe—he gained one of the windows, which, constructed of painted glass, flank the chair of the Vice-President on either side. Here he paused, unable to make more headway. But determined to see Mr. Webster as he spoke, with his knife he made a large hole in one of the panes of the glass; which is still visible as he made it. Many were so placed, as not to be able to see the speaker at all.

The courtesy of Senators accorded to the fairer sex room on the floor—the most gallant of them, their own seats. The gay bonnets and brilliant dresses threw a varied and picturesque beauty over the scene, softening and embellishing it.

Seldom, if ever, has speaker in this or any other country had more powerful incentives to exertion; a subject, the determination of which involved the most important interests, and even duration, of the republic; competitors, unequalled in reputation, ability, or position; a name to make still more glorious, or lose forever; and an audience, comprising not only persons of this country most eminent in intellectual greatness, but representatives of other nations, where the art of eloquence had flourished for ages. All the soldier seeks in opportunity was here.

Mr. Webster perceived, and felt equal to, the destinies of the moment. The very greatness of the hazard exhilarated him. His spirits rose with the occasion. He awaited the time of onset with a stern and impatient joy. He felt, like the war-horse of the Scriptures,—who " paweth in the valley, and rejoiceth in his strength: who goeth on to meet the armed men, —who sayeth among the trumpets, Ha, ha! and who smelleth the battle afar off, the thunder of the captains and the shouting."

A confidence in his own resources, springing from no vain estimate of his power, but the legitimate offspring of previous severe mental discipline sustained and excited him. He had guaged his opponents, his subject and *himself*.

He was too, at this period, in the very prime of manhood. He had reached middle age—an era in the life of man, when the faculties, physical or intellectual, may be supposed to attain their fullest organization, and most perfect development. Whatever there was in him of intellectual energy and vitality, the occasion, his full life and high ambition, might well bring forth.

He never rose on an ordinary occasion to address an ordinary audience more self-possessed. There was no tremulousness in his voice nor manner; nothing hurried, nothing simulated. The calmness of superior strength was visible everywhere; in countenance, voice and bearing. A deep-seated conviction of the extraordinary character of the emergency, and of his ability to control it, seemed to possess him wholly. If an observer, more than ordinarily keen-sighted, detected at times something like exultation in his eye, he presumed it sprang from the excitement of the moment, and the anticipation of victory.

The anxiety to hear the speech was so intense, irrepressible, and universal, that no sooner had the Vice-President assumed the chair, than a motion was made and unanimously carried, to postpone the ordinary preliminaries of Senatorial action, and to take up immediately the consideration of the resolution.

Mr. Webster rose and addressed the Senate. His exordium is known by heart, everywhere: "Mr. President, when the mariner has been tossed, for many days, in thick weather, and on an unknown sea, he naturally avails himself of the first pause in the storm, the earliest glance of the sun, to take his latitude, and ascertain how far the elements have driven him from his true course. Let us imitate this prudence; and before we float further, on the waves of this debate, refer to the point from which we departed, that we may, at least, be able to form some conjecture where we now are. I ask for the reading of the resolution."

There wanted no more to enchain the attention. There was a spontaneous, though silent, expression of eager approbation, as the orator concluded these opening remarks. And while the clerk read the resolution, many attempted the impossibility of getting nearer the speaker. Every head was inclined closer towards him, every ear turned in the direction of his voice—and that deep, sudden, mysterious silence followed, which always attends fulness of emotion. From the sea of upturned faces before him, the orator beheld his thoughts reflected as from a mirror. The varying countenance, the suffused eye, the earnest smile, and ever-attentive look assured him of his audience's entire sympathy. If among his hearers there were those who affected at first an indifference to his glowing thoughts and fervent periods, the difficult mask was soon laid aside, and profound, undisguised, devoted attention followed. In the earlier part of his speech, one of his principal opponents seemed deeply engrossed in the careful perusal of a newspaper he held before his face; but this, on nearer approach, proved to be *upside down*. In truth, all, sooner or later, voluntarily, or in spite of themselves, were wholly carried away by the eloquence of the orator.

One of the happiest retorts ever made in a forensic controversy was his application of Hayne's comparison of the ghost of the "murdered coalition" to the ghost of Banquo:

"Sir, the honorable member was not, for other reasons, entirely happy in his allusions to the story of Banquo's murder, and Banquo's ghost. It was not, I think, the friends, but the enemies of the murdered Banquo, at whose bidding his spirit would not *down*. The honorable gentleman is fresh in his reading of the English classics, and can put me right if I am wrong; but, according to my poor recollection, it was at those who had begun with caresses, and ended with foul and treacherous murder, that the gory locks were shaken! The ghost of Banquo, like that of Hamlet was, an honest ghost. It disturbed no innocent man. It knew where its appearance would strike terror, and who would cry out, a ghost! It made itself visible in the right quarter, and compelled the guilty, and the conscience-smitten, and none others, to start, with,

> "'Pr'ythee, see there! behold! look! lo,
> If I stand here, I saw him!'

THEIR eyeballs were seared (was it not so, sir?) who had thought to shield themselves, by concealing their own hand, and laying the imputation of the crime on a low and hireling agency in wickedness; who had vainly attempted to stifle the workings of their own coward consciences, by ejaculating, through white lips and chattering teeth, "Thou canst not say I did it!" I have misread the great poet if those who had no way partaken in the deed of death, either found that they were, or *feared that they should be*, pushed from their stools by the ghost of the slain, or exclaimed, to a spectre created by their own fears, and their own remorse, "Avaunt! and quit our sight!"

There was a smile of appreciation upon the faces all around, at this most felicitous use of another's illustration—this turning one's own witness against him—in which Col. Hayne good humoredly joined.

As the orator carried out the moral of Macbeth, and proved by the example of that deep-thinking, intellectual, but insanely-ambitious character, how little of substantial good or permanent power was to be secured by a devious and unblessed policy, he turned his eye with a significance of expression, full of prophetic revelation upon the Vice-President, reminding him that those who had foully removed Banquo had placed

> "A barren sceptre in their gripe,
> *Thence to be wrenched by an unlineal hand,*
> *No son of theirs succeeding.*"

Every eye of the whole audience followed the direction of his own—and witnessed the changing countenance and visible agitation of Mr. Calhoun.

Surely, no prediction ever met a more rapid or fuller confirmation, even to the very manner in which the disaster was accomplished. Within a few brief months, the political fortunes of the Vice-President, at this moment seemingly on the very point of culmination, had sunk so low, there were none so poor to do him reverence.

Whether for a moment a presentiment of the approaching crisis in his fate, forced upon his mind by the manner and language of the speaker, cast a gloom over his countenance, or some other cause, it is impossible to say; but his brow grew dark, nor for some time did his features recover their usual impassibility.

The allusion nettled him,—the more as he could not but witness the effect it produced upon others—and made him restless. He seemed to seek an opportunity to break in upon the speaker; and later in the day, as Mr. Webster was exposing the gross and ludicrous inconsistencies of South Carolina politicians, upon the subject of Internal Improvements, he interrupted him with some eagerness: "Does the chair understand the gentleman from Massachusetts to say that the person now occupying the chair of the Senate has changed his opinions on this subject?" To this, Mr. Webster replied immediately, and good-naturedly: "From nothing ever said to me, sir, have I had reason to know of any change in the opinions of the person filling the chair of the Senate. If such change has taken place, I regret it."*

* Mr. Calhoun's interruption was un-Parliamentary, or rather, un-Senatorial. The Vice-President is not a member of the Senate, and has no voice in it save for the preservation of order and enforcement of the rules. He cannot participate otherwise either in the debates or proceedings. He is simply the presiding officer of the Senate—having no vote in its affairs save on a tie. Had Mr. Webster made a direct, unmistakeable allusion to him, Mr. Calhoun still could have replied through a friendly Senator, or the press. On this occasion he was too much excited to attend to the etiquette of his position. His feelings and his interest in the question made him forgetful of his duty.

Those who had doubted Mr. Webster's ability to cope with and overcome his opponents were fully satisfied of their error before he had proceeded far in his speech. Their fears soon took another direction. When they heard his sentences of powerful thought, towering in accumulative grandeur, one above the other, as if the orator strove, Titan-like, to reach the very heavens themselves, they were giddy with an apprehension that he would break down in his flight. They dared not believe, that genius, learning, any intellectual endowment however uncommon, that was simply mortal, could sustain itself long in a career seemingly so perilous. They feared an Icarian fall.

Ah ! who can ever forget, that was present to hear, the tremendous, the *awful* burst of eloquence with which the orator spoke of the *Old Bay State !* or the tones of deep pathos in which the words were pronounced :

" Mr. President, I shall enter on no encomium upon Massachusetts. There she is—behold her, and judge for yourselves. There is her history : the world knows it by heart. The past, at least, is secure. There is Boston, and

Sometime later than this, after a rupture had taken place between Gen. Jackson and himself, Mr. Forsyth, of Georgia, on being interrupted by some (as he thought) uncalled for question or remark, rebuked him in an emphatic manner for violation of official etiquette. Mr. Van Buren, who ousted and succeeded him, always remained silent, placid, imperturbable in his seat, however personal or severe the attack upon him ;—and no Vice-President since his day has ever attempted to interfere with the discussions of the Senate.

Concord, and Lexington, and Bunker Hill—and there they will remain forever. The bones of her sons, falling in the great struggle for independence, now lie mingled with the soil of every State, from New England to Georgia ; and there they will lie forever. And, sir, where American Liberty raised its first voice ; and where its youth was nurtured and sustained, there it still lives, in the strength of its manhood and full of its original spirit. If discord and disunion shall wound it—if party strife and blind ambition shall hawk at and tear it—if folly and madness—if uneasiness, under salutary and necessary restraint—shall succeed to separate it from that Union, by which alone its existence is made sure, it will stand, in the end, by the side of that cradle in which its infancy was rocked : it will stretch forth its arm with whatever of vigor it may still retain, over the friends who gather round it ; and it will fall at last, if fall it must, amidst the proudest monuments of its own glory, and on the very spot of its origin."

What New England heart was there but throbbed with vehement, tumultuous, irrepressible emotion, as he dwelt upon New England sufferings, New England struggles, and New England triumphs during the war of the Revolution ? There was scarcely a dry eye in the Senate ; all hearts were overcome ; grave judges and men grown old in dignified life turned aside their heads, to conceal the evidences of their emotion.*

* Gen. Washington said that the New England troops came better

In one corner of the gallery was clustered a group of Massachusetts men. They had hung from the first moment upon the words of the speaker, with feelings variously but always warmly excited, deepening in intensity as he proceeded. At first, while the orator was going through his exordium, they held their breath and hid their faces, mindful of the savage attack upon him and New England, and the fearful odds against him, her champion ;—as he went deeper into his speech, they felt easier ; when he turned Hayne's flank on Banquo's ghost, they breathed freer and deeper. But now, as he alluded to Massachusetts, their feelings were strained to the highest tension ; and when the orator, concluding his encomium upon the land of their birth, turned, intentionally, or otherwise, his burning eye full upon them—*they shed tears like girls !*

No one who was not present can understand the excitement of the scene. No one, who was, can give an adequate description of it. No word-painting can convey the deep, intense enthusiasm,—the reverential attention, of that vast assembly—nor limner transfer to canvass their earnest, eager, awe-struck countenances. Though language were as subtile and flexible as thought, it still would be impossible to represent the full idea of the scene. There is something intangible in an emotion, which cannot be transferred. The nicer shades of feeling elude pursuit. Every description, therefore,

clothed into the field, were as orderly there, and fought as well, if not better, than any troops on the continent.

of the occasion, seems to the narrator himself most tame, spiritless, unjust.

Much of the instantaneous effect of the speech arose, of course, from the orator's delivery—the tones of his voice, his countenance, and manner.* These die mostly with the occasion that calls them forth—the impression is lost in the attempt at transmission from one mind to another. They can only be described in general terms. "Of the effectiveness of Mr. Webster's manner, in many parts," says Mr. Everett, "it would be in vain to attempt to give any one not present the faintest idea. It has been my fortune to hear some of the ablest speeches of the greatest living orators on both sides of the water, but I must confess, I never heard anything which

* The personal appearance of Mr. Webster has been a theme of frequent discussion. He was at the time this speech was delivered twenty years younger than now. Time had not thinned nor bleached his hair: it was as dark as the raven's plumage, surmounting his massive brow in ample folds. His eye, always dark and deep-set, enkindled by some glowing thought, shone from beneath his sombre, overhanging brow like lights, in the blackness of night, from a sepulchre. It was such a countenance as Salvator Rosa delighted to paint.

No one understood, or understands, better than Mr. Webster the philosophy of dress: what a powerful auxiliary it is to speech and manner, when harmonizing with them. On this occasion he appeared in a blue coat and buff vest,—the Revolutionary colors of buff and blue;—with a white cravat;—a costume, than which none is more becoming to his face and expression. This courtly particularity of dress adds no little to the influence of his manner and appearance.

so completely realized my conception of what Demosthenes was when he delivered the Oration for the Crown."

Assuredly, Kean nor Kemble, nor any other masterly delineator of the human passions ever produced a more powerful impression upon an audience, or swayed so completely their hearts. This was *acting*,—not *to* the life,—but life itself.

No one ever looked the orator, as he did—"*os humerosque deo similis*," in form and feature how like a god. His countenance spake no less audibly than his words. His manner gave new force to his language. As he stood swaying his right arm, like a huge tilt-hammer, up and down, his swarthy countenance lighted up with excitement, he appeared amid the smoke, the fire, the thunder of his eloquence, like Vulcan in his armory forging thoughts for the Gods!

The human face never wore an expression of more withering, relentless scorn, than when the orator replied to Hayne's allusion to the "murdered coalition." "It is," said Mr. W., "the very cast-off slough of a polluted and shameless press. Incapable of further mischief, it lies in the sewer, lifeless and despised. It is not now, sir, in the power of the honorable member to give it dignity or decency, by attempting to elevate it, and introduce it into the Senate. He cannot change it from what it is—an object of general disgust and scorn. On the contrary, the contact, if he choose to touch it, is more likely to drag him down, down to the place where it lies itself." He looked, as he spoke these words, as if the thing he alluded to was too mean for scorn itself—and the sharp, stinging enunciation made the words still more withering. The audience seemed relieved,—so crushing was the expression of his face which they held on to, as 'twere, spellbound,—when he turned to other topics.

The good-natured yet provoking irony with which he described the imaginary though life-like scene of direct collision between the marshalled array of South Carolina under Gen. Hayne on the one side, and the officers of the United States on the other, nettled his opponent even more than his severer satire ; it seemed so ridiculously true. Col. Hayne enquired, with some degree of emotion, if the gentleman from Massachusetts intended any *personal* imputation by such remarks ? To which Mr. Webster replied, with perfect good humor : " Assuredly not—just the reverse."

The variety of incident during the speech, and the rapid fluctuation of passions, kept the audience in continual expectation, and ceaseless agitation. There was no chord of the heart the orator did not strike, as with a master-hand. The speech was a complete drama of comic and pathetic scenes ; one varied excitement ; laughter and tears gaining alternate victory.

A great portion of the speech is strictly argumentative ; an exposition of constitutional law. But grave as such portion necessarily is, severely logical, abounding in no fancy or episode, it engrossed throughout the undivided attention of every intelligent hearer. Abstractions, under the glowing genius of the orator, acquired a beauty, a vitality, a power to thrill the blood and enkindle the affections, awakening into earnest activity many a dormant faculty. His ponderous syllables had an energy, a vehemence of meaning in them that fascinated, while they startled. His thoughts in their statuesque beauty merely would have gained all critical judgment; but he realized the antique fable, and warmed the marble into life. There was a sense of power in his language,—of power withheld and suggestive of still greater power,—that subdued, as by a spell of mystery, the hearts of all. For power, whether intellectual or physical, produces in its earnest development a feeling closely allied to awe. It was never more felt than on this occasion. It had entire mastery. The sex, which is said to love it best and abuse it most, seemed as much or more carried away than the sterner one. Many who had entered the hall with light, gay thoughts, anticipating at most a pleasurable excitement, soon became deeply interested in the speaker and his subject—surrendered him their entire heart; and, when the speech was over, and they left the hall, it was with sadder perhaps, but, surely, with far more elevated and ennobling emotions.

The exulting rush of feeling with which he went through the peroration threw a glow over his countenance, like inspiration. Eye, brow, each feature, every line of the face seemed touched, as with a celestial fire. All gazed as at something more than human. So Moses might have appeared to the awe-struck Israelites as he emerged from the dark clouds and thick smoke of Sinai, his face all radiant with the breath of divinity!

The swell and roll of his voice struck upon the ears of the spell-bound audience, in deep and melodious cadence, as waves upon the shore of the "far-resounding" sea. The Miltonic grandeur of his words was the fit expression of his thought and raised his hearers up to his theme. His voice, exerted to its utmost power, penetrated every recess or corner of the Senate—penetrated even the ante-rooms and stairways, as he pronounced in deepest tones of pathos these words of solemn significance: "When my eyes shall be turned to behold, for the last time, the sun in heaven, may I not see him shining on the broken and dishonored fragments of a once glorious Union; on States dissevered, discordant, belligerent! on a land rent with civil feuds, or drenched, it may be, in fraternal blood! Let their last feeble and lingering glance rather behold the gorgeous ensign of the Republic, now known and honored throughout the earth, still full high advanced,*

* Mr. Webster may have had in his mind, when speaking of the gorgeous ensign of the Republic, Milton's description of the imperial banner in the lower regions, floating across the immensity of space:

> "Who forthwith from the glittering staff unfurl'd
> The imperial ensign; which, *full high advanced*
> Shone like a meteor streaming to the wind,
> With gems and golden lustre rich imblaz'd,
> Seraphic arms and trophies; all the while
> Sonorous metal blowing martial sounds:"

its arms and trophies streaming in their original lustre, not a stripe erased nor polluted, not a single star obscured, bearing for its motto no such miserable interrogatory as, "What is all this worth?" Nor those other words of delusion and folly, Liberty first and Union afterwards; but everywhere, spread all over in characters of living light, blazing on all its ample folds, as they float over the sea and over the land, and in every wind under the whole heavens, that other sentiment, dear to every American heart, LIBERTY AND UNION, NOW AND FOREVER, ONE AND INSEPARABLE!"

The speech was over, but the tones of the orator still lingered upon the ear, and the audience, unconscious of the close, retained their positions. The agitated countenance, the heaving breast, the suffused eye attested the continued influence of the spell upon them. Hands that in the excitement of the moment had sought each other, still remained closed in an unconscious grasp. Eye still turned to eye, to receive and repay mutual sympathy;—and everywhere around seemed forgetfulness of all but the orator's presence and words.

When the Vice-President, hastening to dissolve the spell, angrily called to order! order! There never was a deeper stillness—not a movement, not a gesture had been made,—not a whisper uttered—order! Silence could almost have

And this in its turn is borrowed from, or suggested by, Tasso's description of the banner of the Crusades, when first unfolded in Palestine—which the inquisitive reader may find, if he choose, in "Jerusalem Delivered."

heard itself, it was so supernaturally still. The feeling was too overpowering, to allow expression, by voice or hand. It was as if one was in a trance, all motion paralyzed.

But the descending hammer of the Chair awoke them, with a start—and with one universal, long-drawn, deep breath, with which the overcharged heart seeks relief,—the crowded assembly broke up and departed.

The New-England men walked down Pennsylvania avenue that day, after the speech, with a firmer step and bolder air—"pride in their port, defiance in their eye." You would have sworn they had grown some inches taller in a few hours' time. They devoured the way, in their stride. They looked every one in the face they met, fearing no contradiction They swarmed in the streets, having become miraculously multitudinous. They clustered in parties, and fought the scene over one hundred times that night. Their elation was the greater, by reaction. It knew no limits, or choice of expression. Not one of them but felt he had gained a personal victory. Not one, who was not ready to exclaim, with gushing eyes, in the fulness of gratitude, "Thank God, I too am a Yankee!"

In the evening General Jackson held a levee at the White House. It was known, in advance, that Mr. Webster would attend it, and hardly had the hospitable doors of the house been thrown open, when the crowd that had filled the Senate-chamber in the morning rushed in and occupied the rooms.

Persons a little more tardy in arriving found it almost impossible to get in, such a crowd oppressed the entrance.

Before this evening, the General had been the observed of all observers. His military and personal reputation, official position, gallant bearing, and courteous manners, had secured him great and merited popularity. His receptions were always gladly attended by large numbers—to whom he was himself the object of attraction.

But on this occasion, the room in which he received his company was deserted, as soon as courtesy to the President permitted. Mr. Webster, it was whispered, was in the East Room, and thither the whole mass hurried.

He stood almost in the centre of the room, hemmed in by eager crowds, from whom there was no escape, all pressing to get nearer to him. He seemed but little exhausted by the intellectual exertion of the day, severe as it had been. The flush of excitement still lingered and played upon his countenance, gilding and beautifying it, like the setting sun its accompanying clouds.

All were eager to get a sight at him. Some stood on tiptoe, and some even mounted the chairs of the room. Many were presented to him. The dense crowd, entering and retiring, moved round him, renewing the order of their ingression and egression, continually. One would ask his neighbor: "Where, which is Webster?"—"There, don't you see him—that dark, swarthy man, with a great deep eye and heavy brow—that's Webster." No one was obliged to make a second inquiry.

In another part of the room was Col. Hayne. He, too, had had his day of triumph, and received congratulations. His friends even now contended that the contest was but a drawn-battle, no full victory having been achieved on either side. There was nothing in his own appearance this evening to indicate the mortification of defeat. With others, he went up and complimented Mr. Webster on his brilliant effort ;* and no one, ignorant of the past struggle, could have supposed that they had late been engaged in such fierce rivalry.

* It was said at the time, that, as Col. Hayne approached Mr. Webster to tender his congratulations, the latter accosted him with the usual courtesy, "How are you, this evening, Col. Hayne?" and that Col. Hayne replied, good-humoredly, "*None the better for you, sir!*"

CHAPTER VII.

Colonel Hayne occupied himself diligently in taking notes while Mr. Webster spoke, and replied, in a speech of about half an hour, to Mr. Webster's constitutional opinions. The speech reported contained a great deal more than the one delivered; the great importance of the question making it desirable, in Colonel Hayne's opinion, that arguments should be supplied, which he had been obliged, from want of time, to omit in the debate.

Mr. Webster immediately replied in a summary re-statement of his argument; "of which the parallel, says Mr. Everett, "as a compact piece of reasoning, will not readily be found." Mr. Adams pronounced it even superior to the one that preceded it. It fills less than three pages of the Congressional Debates, while Hayne's, to which it was a reply, occupies nineteen.

The manner in which the Great Speech, as the second in point of time is called, to distinguish it from the one that preceded and the one that followed it, came before the public, it may not be uninteresting to know. Mr. Clayton, of Delaware, and Judge Burnett, of Ohio,—then Senators,—called the morning of the speech upon Mr. Gales, the senior editor of the *National Intelligencer*, and at that time Mayor of the city of Washington, and requested him to undertake the reporting of the speech. Mr. Gales was known to be one of the best writers of the English language connected with our national literature, and more capable than almost any one else, of understanding and recording the peculiar merits of Mr. Webster's style. Notwithstanding the engrossing nature of his avocations, he assented to the request. He made a stenographic report of the speech, which Mrs. Gales wrote out at large. Her copy was sent to Mr. Webster, and by him revised the same evening.

The demand for the speech was immense. The *National Intelligencer* of May, 1830, said—" The demand for copies of Mr. Webster's speech in what has been called the Great Debate in the Senate, has been unprecedented. We are just completing an edition of 20,000 copies, which, added to former editions, will make an aggregate of nearly 40,000 copies that have been printed at this office alone."

Pamphlet editions too were struck off in thousands ; not in Washington alone, but elsewhere. A very large edition was printed in Boston, containing Colonel Hayne's speech also. A proposal was made to the friends of Colonel Hayne to publish a joint edition for distribution throughout the country; this liberal offer was however declined on their part.

Never before, in this or any other country, did any speech gain such rapid and general circulation.

The debate still continued after the conclusion of the contest between Mr. Webster and Colonel Hayne, for weeks and even months. Commencing early in January, it dragged on, with fitful interruptions, till the 21st of May, on which day Colonel Benton, who had in truth provoked it, brought it to a close. The excitement gradually subsided, till, towards the end of the debate, the speakers addressed " empty boxes." Benton, Woodbury, Grundy, Rowan and Livingston, each attempted, more or less creditably, a reply to Mr. Webster's positions. But their eloquence seemed cold, their arguments ineffective, after Mr. Webster's; spectators became indifferent—

> " As in a theatre, the eyes of men,
> After a well-graced actor leaves the stage,
> Are idly bent on him that enters next,
> Thinking his prattle to be tedious."

The *United States Telegraph*, Mr. Calhoun's putative organ, in speaking of " the Great Debate in the Senate," said in the paper of the 8th of February—" The importance of this debate must be apparent to all. It is deeply felt here. The Senators who have spoken, and those who will speak, discharge a great and sacred duty to their country. It is not a holiday debate, but a real and eventful contest for the safety of the States, and the counteraction of the most *daring* schemes for the recovery of lost power, that our country has ever witnessed. Mr. Webster has brought it forward, but he lacks *courage* to breast the storm which he has excited. He has not been seen in the Senate since, except to vote for his party. He depends upon his speech, which is to go forth, North and West, to rally all that can be collected in the crusade against the States, against the South, and against the present administration. It must not go forth unanswered, and it will not."

The answers came, "thick as autumnal leaves that strew the brooks in Vallambrosa;" and as rapidly disappeared. Few even of well-informed politicians have read them; while, to the general student, they are mostly wholly unknown. Not that they were without talent; some possessed far more than ordinary ability, but they have all been forgotten in the superior interest excited by Mr. Webster's effort.

Mr. Woodbury's speech, as an argument, perhaps, followed Colonel Hayne's in ability. He took care to avoid, with the sagacity that distinguishes his character, the extreme doctrine of his southern ally. He would not acknowledge the constitutional right of a State to prevent the execution of a law of the United States believed by such State to be unconstitutional, but referred opposition to the inalienable right of resistance to oppression. In truth, he diverged but little from the line of argument adopted by Mr. Webster.

His speech was grateful to the *juste milieu* of the Democratic party in the Senate and the country. It also particularly pleased the distinguished Senator from Missouri. When Mr. Woodbury had concluded, Colonel Benton rose, and extending his right hand over the head of the Granite Senator, much like a pope or cardinal pronouncing benediction, exclaimed in a loud voice —"Yes, this is Peter, and this Peter is the rock on which the church of New-England democracy shall be built;" and then added in a low tone, not supposed to be intended for the hearing of the Senate—" and the gates of Hell shall not prevail against him."

Such things as this give a relief to the grave and solemn proceedings of the august Senate.

Col. Benton himself spoke four days. He did not go into an elaborate argument upon the relative powers of the States and the Federal Government*—in which his success pro-

* Col. Benton, however, gave the Senate his opinion upon the subject which coincided too nearly with Mr. Hayne's; the best answer to it is to be found in his own words, as spoken in the Senate of the United States, on the third day of January last. Speaking of his constituents, he says: "They abide the law when it comes, be it what it may, subject to the decision of the ballot-box and the judiciary.

"I concur with the people of Missouri in this view of their duty, and believe it to be the only course consistent with the terms and intentions of our Constitution, and the only one which can save this Union from the fate of all the confederacies which have successively appeared and disappeared in the history cf nations. Anarchy among the members and not tyranny in the head, has been the rock on which all such confederacies have split. The authors of our present form of government knew the danger of this rock, and they endeavored to provide against it. They formed a union—not a league—a Federal Legislature to act upon persons, not upon States; and they provided peaceful remedies for all the questions which could arise between the people and the government. They provided a federal judiciary to execute the federal laws when

bably would have been fully equal to that of Col. Hayne or Mr. Woodbury—but rather indulged the Senate with a history of parties during the late war with Great Britain, and also with a review of the action of Congress upon the subject of the public lands. His speech for one so long and various was not uninteresting.

Something perhaps should be said of the person who, ignorant of its explosive qualities, threw this bomb into the Senate.

No man assuredly ever achieved immortality easier than Mr. Foote, of Conn. As the author of the Resolution, he will go down to the latest posterity, while the names of many who shared in the debate will be lost in the early part of the journey; are indeed even now almost forgotten.

He was a man no otherwise distinguished, and perhaps in-

found to be constitutional, and popular elections to repeal them when found to be bad. They formed a government in which the law and popular will, and not the sword, was to decide questions; and they looked upon the first resort to the sword for the decision of such questions as the death of the Union. The old confederation was a league, with a legislature acting upon sovereignties, without power to enforce its decrees, and without union except at the will of the parties. It was powerless for government and a rope of sand for union. It was to escape from that helpless and tottering government that the present Constitution was formed."

Such a full recantation of political heresy required a degree of magna nimity and moral courage seldom found. Any man may commit errors —but few, like the distinguished Senator from Missouri, have the hardihood to acknowledge and the manliness to correct them.

capable of any particular distinction. Amiable in private life, respectable but never eminent in public, of no ill-regulated ambition, nor eccentric vanity, he was one of the last to have been suspected of designing to give character or intellectual vitality to thought or action. And surely no man was more surprised than himself at the formidable consequences of his innocent act. What he had proposed as a harmless enquiry became through the agency of others the immediate cause of an animated, fiery discussion; in which personalities were given and retorted; provocations maliciously put forth, and indignantly thrown back; and argument the most profound, eloquence the most impassioned, embodied in language the most chaste and sublime, involved in the discussion of the most momentous interests. He was the most confounded at his own importance. To use the language of Sir Walter Scott, he felt "the terrors of a child, who has, in heedless sport, put in motion some powerful piece of machinery; and while he beholds wheels revolving, chains clashing, cylinders rolling around him, is equally astonished at the tremendous powers which his weak agency has called into action, and terrified for the consequences which he is compelled to await without the possibility of averting them." But it must not be inferred from the mention of no other name, that Mr. Webster alone of the Opposition Senators participated in this debate. Such an opinion would do injustice to the history of the affair. Messrs. Sprague and Holmes, of Maine, Barton, of Missouri, Johnston, of La., Clayton, of Delaware, and Robbins, of Rhode

Island, with others, made speeches, and good speeches. Mr. Clayton made a most able argument, full of historical research, upon the various duties and powers of the co-ordinate branches of the Government.

Barton, of Missouri, severely castigated his colleague, filling the part in the drama declined by Mr. Webster. He was a man, like Swift, of coarse invective, and coarser humor. Equal to Randolph in bitterness, he excelled even that dreaded satirist in personal vituperation. Of an original and eccentric mind, a rapid though not profound thinker, his speeches often produced an effect, more than proportioned, perhaps, to their intrinsic merit.

While he was speaking on this occasion, the Vice-President called him to order, for using "expressions inadmissible in a deliberative body." Circumstances, it is said, alter cases. When John Randolph, a few years previous, was transgressing not merely the rules of debate but of courtesy, in calling the President a Puritan, and the Secretary of State a black-leg, Mr. Calhoun refused to call him to order, on the ground that it was his sole office to preside over the deliberations of the Senate, and not to keep order in it. Mr. Barton, however, could now be reprimanded though much less guilty.

Mr. Sprague, of Maine, made an excellent speech in defence of New England, temperate and conclusive. Other Senators of the anti-Jackson party distinguished themselves more or less in the debate. Some, who did not speak, refrained, not through lack of ability, but from a conviction that the occasion did not need their voices. Chambers, of Maryland, Burnett, of Ohio, Seymour, of Vt., and Ruggles, of Ohio, were equal to any forensic combat. These and others formed a *corps du reserve*, which could have been brought up, when ever the nature of the contest seemed to require their aid.

In speaking of the political and personal friends of Mr. Webster on this occasion, it would be injustice to make no allusion to Mr. Silsbee, of Mass. His position as colleague of Mr. Webster,—the intimacy that subsisted between them,—his character, ability, and influence in the Senate provoke and justify the mention of his name. In this important crisis, he stood manfully by his colleague, gave him advice, aid and sympathy, wholly and devotedly. What the sympathy of an earnest, ardent, capable and experienced friend is worth they can only tell, who have been in exigencies to require it.

Mr. Webster and Mr. Silsbee were colleagues other than in position. They did not represent Massachusetts merely, but the same liberal ideas and principles. Harmonious in sentiment as in action, they consulted together under no restriction of official etiquette, but freely, frankly, fraternally. It was of much advantage to Mr. Webster, to be able to lean upon such a man, in such an emergency; to feel sure of warm sympathy, unbounded friendship, and untiring zeal, while he battled against such odds, for reputation and political existence.

There was no envy in Mr. Silsbee; no malice; no jealous repining at another's superiority. His colleague, he knew, towered above him, and overshadowed him. But he was not one of the sickly plants that languish in the shade. He had inherent vitality enough, constitutional vigor enough, to live, and grow strong and vigorous, without incessant sunshine.

The profession to which he was educated did not insist upon his being an orator. And yet few, trained to forensic pursuits, knew better to express their meaning; or could reach, by shorter path, the understanding of their auditors, and gain so entirely their convictions. The sincerity of his purpose gave force and transparency to his language. No man in the Senate enjoyed, or deserved, more respect.

Mr. Webster was not only assailed in the Senate by the chiefs of the administration party, but by the democratic press, generally throughout the country. The metropolitan newspaper,—the *U. S. Telegraph*,—whose editor was printer to the Senate, attacked him with relentless malice. This kind of assault troubled him most, as he had no means of meeting or repelling it. Some action in the matter, however, he thought demanded by his position as Senator, and that of the editor as an officer of the Senate. Accordingly, on the 28th of January he rose in his seat in the Senate and said: "A newspaper has been put into my hands this morning, purporting to be printed and published in this city by Duff Green, who is printer to the Senate. In this, I find an article referring to the debate in the Senate yesterday; and in that article, among other statements equally false, it is said, that Mr. Webster contended that 'the National Government was established by the people, who had imparted to it unlimited powers over the States and Constitution.'

"I am of opinion that we ought to leave our seats altogether, or protect ourselves from atrocious and wilful calumnies, committed by persons who are admitted on this floor, and receive from our hands large disbursements of public money. It becomes us to yield our places here to men of better spirit and go home, or show that we are not to be bullied or slandered out of a free and full exercise of our functions."

He then gave notice that on a similar occurrence of a similar offence, he should make a specific motion.

His opponents finding where they could assail him with the most injury to him and impunity to themselves reiterated the charges against him, in the Telegraph, with additional virulence. Mr. Webster, in consequence, submitted the following resolution to the Senate : "*Resolved*, That the Senate will on the fourth day of February next proceed to the choice of a printer to the Senate." This resolution, however, he consented soon after, on the advice of friends, to withdraw ; and no farther action was had on the matter.

If Mr. Webster needed aught else to satisfy his ambition than the proud consciousness of having ably discharged his duty to his country, the warm testimonials of grateful admiration that poured in upon him from the most distinguished individuals, in every part of the Union, might have been considered fully sufficient. Massachusetts,—to whose name he has erected a monument no more perishable than her soil,—came eagerly forward to evince her earnest gratitude. The most eminent in the State, for piety, learning, or public worth, sent him letters of thanks for the great service he had rendered the State and the Union—" their children's children"—they wrote —" would bless him, as they did, to the latest posterity." Resolutions of a majority of both branches of the Legislature, and of numerous assemblies throughout the State and New England, all expressive of the deepest gratitude for his successful vindication of the name and character of the State and New England from undeserved reproach, were forwarded to him, in due time.

Nor was praise of his effort confined to his State or New England. It was general, as the service he had performed to his country. His exposition and defence of the Constitution drew forth the expression of thanks from every quarter. " The ability with which the great argument is treated"—writes the Hon. William Gaston, formerly a distinguished member of Congress from North Carolina—" the patriotic fervor with which the Union is asserted, give you claim to the gratitude of every one who loves his country and regards the Constitution as its best hope and surest stay. My engrossing occupations leave me little leisure for any correspondence except on business,—but I have resolved to seize a moment to let you know that with us there is scarcely a division of opinion among the intelligent portion of the community. All of them, whose understanding or whose conscience are not surrendered to the servitude of faction greet your eloquent efforts with unmixed approbation."

" I congratulate you," writes Mr. Clay, " on the very great addition which you have made, during the session, to your previous high reputation. Your speeches, and particularly in reply to Mr. Hayne, are the theme of praise from every tongue; and I have shared in the delight which all have felt."

Commendation of the speech from persons almost equally distinguished, reached Mr. Webster ; from one, still more so. James Madison, one of the principal framers of the Constitution, and, in safest opinion, its best interpreter, wrote to a friend soon after reading this speech, in warm terms of its ability, its constitutional character, and its " tremendous effect upon the doctrines of nullification."

There is no such thing as extemporaneous speaking, strictly considered. No man can address an assembly in language worthy to be remembered, without some previous study of his subject. The command of a whole vocabulary will not supply ideas ; verbal fluency is even dangerous to their proper expression. We lose the substance in the shadow.

Certainly, therefore, it will not be contended, that Mr. Webster's entire reply to Col. Hayne was the inspiration of the moment—that he took no thought, before speech, of what he should say. Most undoubtedly, some of the important questions which he discussed on this celebrated occasion had received, previously, his attention and careful consideration.

The Tariff, the Public Lands, and the Constitution, were matters of a too important character not to demand the recognition and deep study of any statesman.

But of what is generally understood by preparation, Mr. Webster had made little: less, perhaps, for an occasion of equal importance, than any orator of ancient or modern times. The orators of antiquity, it is well known, elaborated their sentences no less than their thoughts; were as anxious about a phrase as a sentiment; while those most celebrated of modern days have been also most distinguished for previous study. Burke and Canning, more especially, polished and amended, revised and re-revised, till the original thought was hardly recognizable in its last dress.

Mr. Webster's *brief* on this occasion did not cover one side of a sheet of paper, the major part of it being in relation to the Public Lands; while the most important topic of the speech, that which related to the history and interpretation of the Constitution, was discussed *without a single note.* A fact that seems the more remarkable, when it is recollected that Mr. Webster had never been engaged in the discussion of a Constitutional question at any time in his previous Parliamentary career. It is true, however, that in his professional life he had had occasion to examine and argue some important points of Constitutional Law, as in the Dartmouth College case, and in the steamboat case of *Gibbons* vs. *Ogden*, already alluded to. But these cases, important as they were to the proper settlement of vexed questions, and involving as they do high principles of Constitutional law, did not agitate the delicately-adjusted political relations between the States and the Federal Government. This question was first examined in full in this debate. Undoubtedly, however, Mr. Webster had dwelt upon it before in his mind; the whole force and capacity of it were not opened to him at the moment, like a revelation. He was full of it, and required no promptings and no guides. The mind, contend the metaphysicians, always thinks; and Mr. Webster's, more than other men's, may have been exercised upon such lofty themes as these.

No one can read this speech of his in reply to Hayne, or any or either of his most celebrated productions, without being reminded of scriptural passages. In truth, no writer or speaker of any reputation, of the age, is more imbued with the spirit of Hebrew poetry than Mr. Webster. Those nearest admitted to his intimacy wonld be the readiest to bear testimony to his familiar acquaintance with the literature of the Old Bible. "The hidden treasure of poetry," (I quote from recollection merely) "is the Hebrew books. Few persons remount to the source, to 'Siloa's brook, that flowed fast by the oracle of God.' There is no writer in any language, ancient or modern, more poetical than Habakkuk. In the translation, even, he appears to greater advantage than the heroic poets—than Homer, or those that followed him. In the vernacular, besides the energy of the words there is a rythm, a metre, as much as in the Iliad or Eneid. The translation has not always destroyed it; as take, for instance, the following lines:

'Although the fig-tree shall not blossom,
Neither shall fruit be in the vines;
The labor of the olive shall fail,
And the fields shall yield no meat;
The flock shall be cut off from the fold,
And there shall be no herd in the stalls:
Yet will I rejoice in the Lord, I will joy in the God of my salvation.'

Here now is a regular equiponderance of sentences till you get to the last line, which is double. Then what beautiful and expressive language! 'The labor of the olive!' In what other book will you find an expression of like energy and beauty? The tree itself is, by a bold metaphor, made to contribute, spontaneously, to the wants of man, as if it had thews and muscles, and was capable of action. 'The field shall yield no meat.' What a stronger impression the word 'meat' conveys, than product, or fruit, or any common term. It is true—poetical. It at once gives you the idea of all that maketh glad the heart of man; and the failure of the fields, therefore, falls upon the mind with a heavier gloom.

The whole chapter is sublime. I read it often, and each time with still greater admiration 'The prayer of Habakkuk,' as it is called."

It would be unfair to Mr. Webster to attempt to give his language from remembrance. No author, of another tongue, would suffer more from translation. Some of the strongest expressions, no less than nicer shades of sentiment, would be lost in the transmission. He must be heard to be appreciated.

Those admitted to the intimacy of his conversation, can tell of the eloquent fervor with which he speaks of the inspired writings—how much light he can throw upon a difficult text—how much beauty lend to expressions that would escape all but the eye of genius—what new vigor he can give to the most earnest thoughts—and what elevation to even sublimity. "It would be impossible," says a distinguished orator from another section of the country, "for any one to listen half an hour to Mr. Webster on the Scriptures, and not believe in their inspiration—*or his.*"

But while Mr. Webster's public productions and private conversations attest how deeply he is imbued with the spirit of the Scriptures, neither the one nor the other ever contained the slightest irreverent allusion to any passage in them—anything in the way of illustration, analogy or quotation, that could seem to question their sanctity. He has been scrupulously delicate in this regard; and therein differs widely from most of his contemporaries in public life on this continent: for it is made matter of reproach to us, as a nation, that our public speakers, in Congress particularly, take the grossest liberties with the most sacred texts of the Scriptures—use them to garnish the most ordinary topics, or illustrate their own ignoble pursuits and histories; and, in fact, pay them no more regard than profane books.

It is not so in England. Good taste, if not a religious

sense, avoids any such irreverence. When Lord Plunkett once, in the House of Commons, in speaking of the great anticipations that were entertained of George IV.'s accession to the throne, alluded to it as THE GREAT COMING, the members of the House were shocked, and the speaker felt the rebuke.

CHAPTER VIII.

The same year in which Mr. Webster gained his forensic laurels in the Senate of the United States, secured him also a great professional triumph. All of New England, at that time of sufficient age and capacity to have comprehended it, will recollect the deep, intense sensation produced throughout the community that year by the extraordinary murder of Joseph White, in Salem, Massachusetts, on the night of the 6th of April. The respectability, wealth, and advanced age of the murdered man, the mysterious nature of the midnight murder, the strange and romantic details connected with its perpetration, the relationship of one of the assassins to the victim, and other circumstances of almost equal interest, produced an excitement at the time, which was as deep as it was general, and which has dwelt upon the mind ever since with nearly all the distinctness of its first impression.

A few weeks after the murder, Richard Crowningshield, George Crowningshield, brothers, Joseph J. Knapp, who had married a daughter of the neice of the murdered man, and John Francis Knapp, also brothers, were arrested, on a charge of having perpetrated the murder, and committed for trial. Joseph J. Knapp, soon after his arrest, under promise of favor from the government, was induced to make a full confession of the crime, and of the circumstances attending it. A few days after his disclosure had been made and become known, Richard Crowningshield, who was supposed to have been the principal assassin, committed suicide.

By act of the Legislature, a special session of the Supreme Court was holden at Salem, in July, for the trial of the prisoners. In the ordinary arrangement of the courts, but one week in a year, was allotted for the whole court to sit in that county; and, as in the trial of all capital offences, a majority of the court were required to be present, and as weeks would in all probability be consumed in this trial, but for such interposition of the Legislature, three years would not have been sufficient for the purpose. It was for this reason and not on account of the excitement in the community, and the interest felt in the result, that the special session was ordered.

Before this court, John Francis Knapp was arraigned as principal in the murder, and George Crowningshield and Joseph J. Knapp, accessories.

If the suicide of Richard Crowningshield before the commencement of the trial, added to the already excited state of the public feeling, the unexpected withdrawal of his confession by Joseph J. Knapp, and his refusal, on being called upon, to testify, had no tendency to allay it.

Mr. Webster, upon the request of the prosecuting officers

of the government, appeared as counsel and assisted in the trial.

In the earlier part of his argument to the jury, Mr. Webster said—"Gentlemen, this is a most extraordinary case. In some respects, it has hardly a precedent anywhere; certainly none in our New England history This bloody drama exhibited no suddenly excited ungovernable rage. The actors in it were not surprised by any lion-like temptation springing upon their virtue and overcoming it, before resistance could begin. Nor did they do the deed, to glut savage vengeance, or satiate long settled and deadly hate. It was a cool, calculating, money-making murder. It was all 'hire and salary, not revenge.' It was the weighing of money against life; the counting out of so many pieces of silver, against so many ounces of blood."

In speaking of the supposed self-congratulation of the murderer, as he escapes, unseen by human eye, after the perpetration of the deed, Mr. Webster describes the danger of a fatal secret in language that makes the reader almost feel the consciousness of guilt himself. "It is accomplished. The deed is done. The assassin retreats; retraces his steps to the window, passes out through it as he came in, and escapes. He has done the murder. No eye has seen him, no ear has heard him. The *secret* is his own, and it is safe!

"Ah! gentlemen, that was a dreadful mistake. Such a secret can be safe nowhere. The whole creation of God has neither nook nor corner where the guilty can bestow it, and say it is safe. Not to speak of that eye which glances through all disguises, and beholds everything as in the splendor of noon, such secrets of guilt are never safe from detection, even by men. True it is, generally speaking, that 'murder will out.' True it is, that Providence hath so ordained, and doth so govern things, that those who break the law of heaven, by shedding man's blood, seldom succeed in avoiding discovery. A thousand eyes turn at once to explore every man, every thing, every circumstance, connected with the time and place; a thousand ears catch every whisper; a thousand excited minds intensely dwell on the scene, shedding all their light, and ready to kindle the slightest circumstance into a blaze of discovery. Meanwhile the guilty soul cannot keep its own secret. It is false to itself; or rather, it feels an irresistible impulse of conscience to be true to itself. It labors under its guilty possession, and knows not what to do with it. The human heart was not made for the residence of such an inhabitant. It finds itself preyed upon by a torment which it does not acknowledge to God nor man. A vulture is devouring it, and it can ask no sympathy or assistance, either from heaven or earth. The secret which the murderer possesses soon comes to possess him; and, like the evil spirits of which we read, it overcomes him, and leads him whithersoever it will. He feels it beating at his heart, rising to his throat, and demanding disclosure. He thinks the whole world sees it in his face, reads it in his eyes, and almost hears its workings in the very silence of his thoughts. It has become his master.

It betrays his discretion, it breaks down his courage, it conquers his prudence. When suspicions, from without, begin to embarrass him, and the net of circumstance to entangle him, the fatal *secret* struggles with still greater violence to burst forth. It must be confessed; it *will be* confessed; *there is no refuge from confession but suicide, and suicide* IS *confession.*"

The great difficulty Mr. Webster had to surmount in the case was, the doubt in the minds of the jury, that John Francis Knapp was present in the vicinity at the time of the murder, for the purpose of aiding and abetting it. Richard Crowningshield was the actual perpetrator of the murder; he alone entered the house, and gave the old man his death-wounds. But, by his own act, he was placed beyond the reach of an earthly tribunal; and, unless it was demonstrated to the satisfaction of the jury, that, on the night of the murder, John Francis Knapp was aiding, *in constructive presence*, the accomplishment of the deed, and thus proved a *principal* to it, the three prisoners, however guilty in public opinion and in fact, must have been discharged, since the one indicted as principal being pronounced innocent, the accessories could not of course have been convicted.

The admirable ingenuity of argument by which Mr. Webster led the minds of the jury to this conclusion, is equal to anything of the kind in the annals of the profession. The interpretation he gave to the various and somewhat contradictory evidence upon the subject; the manner in which he combined circumstances at first seemingly independent, dove-tailing them together so that their separation appeared impossible, and the full solution which he returned to the suggested doubts of opposite counsel, in regard to identity of person, &c., rendered Knapp's guilt, in the opinion of the jury, a matter not merely of vehement probability, but absolute necessity.

He was convicted, and his associates also.

The history of the murder is a singular one ; and, were it not that truth is stranger than fiction, would hardly be credited in all of its details.

The first conception of the murder arose, it is said, from the conversation and character of the victim. The idea of murder was not native to those who plotted it ; but from their education, position, and associations, was abhorrent to their minds. They had led somewhat extravagant and reckless lives, it is true, but nothing had been imputed to them indicative of cruel dispositions or hardened consciences. Their victim, in his familiar conversation, to which of course they were admitted—the Knapps at least—was accustomed to speak, with some carelessness of expression, of things worthy of reverence; to profess a doubt of eternal life, and a reckless impatience of this tedious existence. J. J. Knapp, and others, often listening to such talk, began to think of indulging the wishes of the speaker, and finally came to the conclusion, that, as he stood shivering on the brink, seemingly desirous, yet fearing to plunge, it would be no unkindness in them to afford him a little aid.

The murder was committed through a mistake of law.

Some weeks previous to it, Joseph Knapp applied to a lawyer to ascertain the law as to the distribution of the estate of the old gentleman, in case he should die intestate. The lawyer advised him, that the estate would descend to his nephews and neices, his next of kin, *per stirpes*, and not *per capita;* Knapp thence concluded that his mother-in-law, who was a neice of the old gentleman, and sole representative of one of the two branches, would inherit half the estate, which was very large, and that in consequence, it was a matter of great moment that he (Mr. White) should die and leave no will.

The murder was committed too, through a mistake of *fact*, for though the murderers got a will, it was not *the* will. The one destroyed was made sometime before the murder; another was found after the murder, bequeathing the mass of the property to the other branch of the family. This circumstance, of Knapp's not being benefited by the murder, for some time averted the suspicion of his being engaged in it. But when it had been ascertained that he was a party to it, his ignorance of the existence of the second will solved the whole mystery, revealed the motive of the act.

The actual murderer, Richard Crowningshield, was indicted, arrested and committed to close confinement in prison, on the testimony of one who was wholly ignorant of the truth or falsehood of what he testified. Hatch, the witness against him, was a felon imprisoned at New Bedford, at the time the murder was committed; he falsely pretended to be able to testify to material facts. Attorney-General Morton, at the

Supreme Judicial Court which sat in Essex, a few weeks after the murder, moved for a *Habeas Corpus ad Testificandum*, and Hatch was carried in chains to Ipswich, and on his testimony, wholly false, a bill of indictment was found against Richard Crowningsheld and three other persons, who were arrested and committed for trial.

Richard Crowningshield did not despond at first in his imprisonment, because he knew he was charged with the crime on false testimony; but a month after, when he heard that some of his accomplices had turned States' evidence, and disclosed the truth, his heart failed him, as he contemplated the seeming desperateness of his condition, and soon abandoning all for lost, he committed suicide, to escape a public ignominious death; while if he had boldly stood the chances of a trial before a jury, he needs must have been acquitted, notwithstanding all the disclosures, for want of sufficient *legal* testimony—the disclosures, so far as he was concerned, having been mere hearsay, which is not, technically, evidence. But, from want of moral courage, he committed suicide, and suicide was confession.

Joseph J. Knapp, it will be recollected, consented at one time to be States' evidence, and to make a full confession of the whole truth; had he remained steadfast to this compact with the government, he would thereby have saved his own life, and, by his testimony, acquitted his brother Francis. His testimony would have proved that Francis was in Brown-street—the *locale* of the murder—without the knowledge and against the wishes of Richard Crowningshield, and that his sole purpose in going there was to ascertain from him, historically, whether the deed had been done. It was proved at the trial, that Francis was in Brown-street at the time of the murder, and the jury from all the evidence, and in the absence of any proof that he was there for any other purpose than to aid Richard Crowningshield, came to the conclusion, that he was there expressly for that purpose; and, consequently, found him guilty as PRINCIPAL. He was thus convicted for want of his brother's testimony. But this very confession of Joseph Knapp, though withdrawn before trial, and thus, technically, ruled out of court, must have produced some influence upon the minds of the jury disastrous to the defendants. A rule of law could prevent the admission of the testimony into court, but not into the minds of men. This confession revealed certain facts—admitted as evidence through the person to whom they were made known—such as the concealment of the club by which Crowningshield perpetrated the murder, and other auxiliary circumstances, without which it might have been difficult to have obtained conviction. Thus, by his double weakness—first in confessing, and then retracting—Joseph Knapp accomplished his brother's conviction of a crime which was perpetrated for his own benefit.

Some censure at the time was passed upon the conduct of the defence. The eminent counsel, it was thought, committed the fatal error of bringing forward no plan, hypothesis or theory which could admit of the innocence of the accused, but contented himself rather with a kind of guerilla warfare, attacking the positions or witnesses of the other side, in a series of flying skirmishes. A kind of defence, which, in criminal cases, never has succeeded, and probably never will.

It was thought also at the time, that the learned counsel for the defence betrayed a want of professional equanimity, if not courtesy, that they made too many and too lachrymose complaints of the professional aid the prosecuting officer retained on the trial, compelling Mr. Webster to say to the jury, that, "In the course of his whole life, he had never before heard so much said about the particular counsel who happen to be employed; as if it were extraordinary that other counsel than the usual officers of the government should be assisting in the conducting of a case on the part of the government." And that they exhibited, in fine, indications of too captious a spirit, and too irascible temperament.

The opinion in regard to the management of the prosecution was warmly approbatory. It was, indeed, generally admitted that, but for Mr. Webster's masterly argument, a conviction would never have been procured against the prisoners. The earnest and resistless logic, by which he demonstrated the necessity of their guilt, dispelled the doubts which had hung over the case from complicated and contradictory evidence. Their *moral* guilt might have been suspected, their *legal* guilt, without him, could not have been established.

The closing words of his argument, in which he reminds the jury of the obligation they were under to discharge their duty, have been quoted before, but may not be unworthy of repetition here: "A sense of duty pursues us ever. It is omnipresent, like the Deity. If we take to ourselves the wings of the morning and dwell in the utmost parts of the sea, duty performed, or duty violated, is still with us, for our happiness or our misery. If we say the darkness shall cover us, in the darkness as in the light, our obligations are yet with us. We cannot escape their power, nor fly from their presence. They are with us in this life, will be with us at its close; and, in that scene of inconceivable solemnity, which lies yet farther onward, we shall still find ourselves surrounded by the consciousness of duty, to pain us wherever it has been violated, and to console us, so far as God may have given us grace to perform it."

CHAPTER IX.

Soon after the reply to Hayne, the principles of constitutional law evolved therefrom, were put to the severest test. The fatal doctrine of nullification, brought boldly forward in Colonel Hayne's argument, for the first time, gained, during the two years that followed, a strength, and following in a certain section, sufficient to create a feeling of sincere apprehension on the part of the friends of the Union.

The motives of actors we can judge of solely from their revelation in deeds. There is no process, moral or legal, to reach the conscience. As *does* a man, so, to all possible understanding, he *thinks*. The reasons assigned, so liberally and authoritatively at times, for the conduct of public men, by the historian or biographer, are those rather of the writer than actor, in a generality of cases.

The narrator can give facts, from which each intelligent reader for himself is able to draw satisfactory conclusions.

Within a year of the famous controversy between Mr. Webster and Colonel Hayne, Mr. Van Buren and Mr. Forsyth, availing themselves of the fortuitous circumstance of a feminine quarrel in General Jackson's cabinet, to ensure a long-premeditated intention, produced a rupture between General Jackson and Mr. Calhoun; a rupture not only of political but personal relations, and of extremer virulence from the preceding intimacy. General Jackson, alike violent in enmity and friendship, began now to cherish and express feelings of deadly hatred towards his associate in the government.

Mr. Calhoun was necessarily precipitated into opposition to his former political friends. He could not remain in the Democratic party against General Jackson. There was no catholicity unrecognized by the head of the faith. Himself and friends, therefore, found themselves in compulsory hostility to the administration. This hostility, originally personal, became soon, by the operation of natural causes, one of measures and principle. To those who are not accustomed to dwell upon the evolutions of politicians, and notice with what a strange rapidity they are performed, it might appear no little surprising that these two eminent individuals, on taking their latitude after the somewhat long duration of their personal conflict, discovered that each had wandered very far from the course in which he had been moving, and in entirely opposite direction the one to the other. Up to the accession of Mr. Adams to the Presidency, in 1825, Mr. Calhoun had been known as an ardent, sincere and efficient advocate of the liberal powers of the general government, especially as regarded the institution of a protective tariff; while General Jackson, except in Pennsylvania, had been considered as favoring, at least in heart, the theory and policy of Mr. Crawford, the leader of the strict constructionists. But now, their positions were wholly reversed ; Mr. Calhoun contending for the right of each State to oppose the measures of the general government, even to nullification—General Jackson insisting upon a large and liberal interpretation of the Constitution, and the putting down of resistance to the exercise of the powers it grants, by the force of the general government.

The controversy, as is ever the case, became more bitter and violent, from the former friendship between the two most distinguished parties to it. Notwithstanding their endeavors to give it an exclusive character of principle, it could not but be felt there was in it great personal vindictiveness. No terms of reproach, accusation or denunciation were spared on either hand, by the friends of either party towards their opponents ; Calhoun-men and Jackson-men hated each other with a hatred far more unsparing than either felt towards their late political opponents.

In spite of the defection of Mr. Calhoun and his friends, General Jackson was re-elected President, in the fall of 1832, by a large majority over Mr. Clay, the candidate of the Opposition—or, "National Republicans," as they then styled themselves—and Mr. Van Buren, Vice-President ; South Carolina alone of the Southern Democratic States, withholding its vote from the candidates of the Democratic party.

Immediately upon the result of the canvass, the people of that State, urged to temporary phrenzy by their political leaders in and out of Congress, met by delegates in convention, and passed what they called an *ordinance*, establishing new and fundamental principles. This convention overthrew the whole revenue system. It did not limit itself to the acts of 1828 or 1832, but adopted a solemn declaration that, in their State, no taxes should be collected. In this declaration they stated that South Carolina had thrown herself into the breach, and would stand foremost in resistance to the laws of the Union; and they solemnly called upon the citizens of the State to stand by the principles of the ORDINANCE. The Legislature of the State, meeting soon after, ratified this ordinance, and declared the tariff acts unconstitutional, and utterly null and void. It passed an act besides, directing the enlisting and enrollment of volunteers, and advised all the citizens to put themselves in military array.

The excitement in the State became intense. The whole State was in arms, or ready to be so at a moment's warning. A military spirit everywhere prevailed. The blue cockade with the Palmetto button, was almost universally worn, and musters were held every day. The city of Charleston wore the appearance of a military depôt; and it was generally supposed, that the first attempt to enforce the revenue laws of the United States, would produce instantaneous collision between the forces of the general government and of the State.

General Hayne resigned his seat in the Senate of the United States, and was elected Governor of the State, to meet the emergency; and Mr. Calhoun, resigning his office as

Vice-President—three months before its constitutional expiration—succeeded General Hayne in the Senate.

The state of public affairs threatened a fatal crisis. General Jackson, unterrified by the belligerent appearance of South Carolina, determined to enforce the law, at every hazard. His cabinet, indeed, maintained a profound silence in regard to his intentions; but some of his most intimate friends announced that he would immediately employ the naval force of the country, and blockade Charleston. Everywhere, throughout the country, an anxious feverish apprehension of some immediate catastrophe agitated the minds of men.

Early in December Congress met. The vacant chair was filled by the election of Hugh L. White, of Tennessee, as President of the Senate, on the fifth ballot, by a vote of seventeen to fourteen for John Tyler, of Virginia. The Senate was composed as follows:

Maine—John Holmes, Peleg Sprague.

New Hampshire—Samuel Bell, Isaac Hill.

Massachusetts—Nathaniel Silsbee, Daniel Webster.

Rhode Island—N. R. Knight, Asher Robbins.

Connecticut—Samuel A. Foot, Gid. Tomlinson.

New York—Charles E. Dudley, Silas Wright.

New Jersey—Mahlon Dickerson, Theo. Frelinghuysen.

Pennsylvania—Geo. M. Dallas, Wm. Wilkins.

Delaware—John M. Clayton, Arnold Naudain.

Maryland—Ezekiel F. Chambers, Samuel Smith.

Virginia—John Tyler, William C. Rives.

North Carolina—Bedford Brown, Willie P. Mangum.

South Carolina—Stephen D. Miller, John C. Calhoun.

Georgia—Geo. M. Troup, John Forsyth.

Kentucky—Geo. M. Bibb, Henry Clay.

Tennessee—Felix Grundy, Hugh L. White.

Ohio—Thomas Ewing, Benjamin Ruggles.

Louisiana—Josiah S. Johnston, Geo. A. Waggaman.

Indiana—William Hendricks, John Tipton.

Mississippi—Geo. Poindexter, John Black.

Illinois—Elias K. Kane, John M. Robinson.

Alabama—William R. King, Gabriel Moore.

Missouri—Thos H. Benton, Alexander Buckner.

Many of these names have an "odor of nationality" about them; and all of them are transcribed here, in order that those not great in themselves may afford *relief* to the others' greatness.

Mr. Calhoun did not arrive in time to be present at the opening of the Senate. His arrival was awaited with no little impatience. Some apprehension was entertained that he would be arrested on his way, on a charge of treason against the government. General Jackson had indulged in a threat of that kind; and those, who knew he seldom threatened but he meant to do, were in momentary expectation of such an event.

On the 10th of December, appeared General Jackson's celebrated proclamation against nullification Probably, no document ever issued from the Executive Department which gave rise to a more profound sensation. It confounded alike friend and foe of the administration. This State paper was the production of Mr. Livingston, then Secretary of State, though it bears in many pages marks of General Jackson's dictation. His will penetrates every sentence of it. Mr. Webster, in the preceding October, in a speech at Worcester, Massachusetts, had reproached the administration for having done nothing and said nothing, to arrest the revolutionary doctrines of nullification. In this speech we had recapitulated the powers and duties of the general government, as previously defined in his reply to Hayne, and urged the necessity of their exercise. But at the same time, and in equally forcible language, he took ground against the employment of military force. "For one"—he said—"I raise my voice beforehand against the unauthorized employment of military power, and against superseding the authority of the laws, by an armed force, under the pretence of putting down nullification. The President has no authority to blockade Charleston; the President has no authority to employ military force till he shall be duly required so to do by law and by the civil authorities. His duty is to cause the laws to be executed. His duty is to support the civil authority. His duty is, if the laws be resisted, to employ the military force of the country, if necessary, for their support and execution; but to do all this in compliance only with law, and with decisions of the tribunals."

Mr. Webster, on his way to Washington in December, first heard of the proclamation in New Jersey, from a traveller, unknown to him, and to whom he also was unknown, who had just left the metropolis. This person told him, as news, that General Jackson had just issued a proclamation against nullification, "taken altogether from Webster's speech at Worcester."

There certainly is a resemblance—strange indeed, if unintentional—between, not the sentiments alone, but the very language of these two productions.

To General Jackson's proclamation, Governor Hayne issued a counter-proclamation, denouncing the attitude of the general government towards the State of South Carolina, and threatening to resist to the last extremity, the enforcement of its jurisdiction over the citizens of the State.

The "crisis" evidently approached. The United States' troops were concentrated, in some force, at Augusta and Charleston, seemingly for the purpose of repressing any insurrectionary or rebellious movement in the State; while on the other side, equal preparation was made. The militia in certain sections of the State were called out and drilled, muskets were put in order, swords cleaned and sharpened, and depôts of provisions and supplies established. Officers, natives of the State, in the army and navy of the United States contemplated resigning their commissions, and flying to the defence of the State. While some foreign officers, then in the country, actually tendered their services to the governor, against the forces of the general government.

Such, in December, was the aspect of affairs in South Carolina. Civil war had not indeed commenced, and yet all that seemed wanting to bring it on, was but a forcible demonstration from either party. At a great assembly of Nullifiers in Charleston, Mr. Preston, one of the most influential among them, said, among other things equally portentous—"There are sixteen thousand back-countrymen *with arms in their hands and cockades in their hats*, ready to march to our city at a moment's warning, to defend us; and the moment Congress shall pass the laws recommended to the President in relation to our port, I will pour down a torrent of volunteers that shall sweep the myrmidons of the tyrant from the soil of Carolina." There was somewhat of bombast in this language, but, unfortunately too, somewhat of truth. There were many in South Carolina ready and even eager for collision with the United States authorities.

This state of things lasted through December, keeping the entire country in constant agitation. In the meantime, Mr. Calhoun did not make his appearance at Washington; his friends said that he remained to prevent an outbreak in South Carolina; his enemies that he feared to encounter the presence of General Jackson.

At length, the news of his departure from South Carolina, and of his progress towards the metropolis, reached Washington, the latter part of December. At Raleigh, North Carolina, he passed, it was said, New Year's day, waited upon by large crowds of people. A public dinner, on the part of the citizens, was offered to, and urged upon him, which he declined on the ground of his public engagements. Travelling more slowly, than in these days of steam, his approach was heralded from one place to another, and preparation made for his reception. Everywhere he was met with respect, even in places where his principles were obnoxious and his course condemned: for it was thought he was honest in his intentions. The story of his progress through North Carolina and Virginia reaching the capital before him, mitigated to a degree the harshness of the general feeling in that place towards him, and prevented any hostile demonstration, if such had been intended, against him.

It was on the fourth day of January, 1833, he took his seat, for the first time, as Senator of the United States. He had presided, as Vice-President, over the deliberations of the Senate for nearly four years, but had never been otherwise a member of that body.

It was an impressive occasion. The Senate was crowded, to witness the ceremony of his taking the oath of office. He walked in, slowly and deliberately, to his seat. Some went up to him and tendered their congratulations; but many of the Senators held back. With his State almost in open rebellion, and himself, in general opinion, its most turbulent agitator, there were many who entertained towards him any but kind feelings. The idea of disunion was then a monstrous and unnatural idea; it had not become familiarized, and all whose language, even by implication, seemed to advocate or tolerate that project, were held in abhorrence.

More than one Senator present, to whom Mr. Calhoun's assured but not presumptuous manner seemed like a bold defiance of opinion, was ready to exclaim, in the words of Cicero, when he addressed the audacious Cataline—"*Quousque tandem abutere Catalina patientiâ nostrâ? quamdiu etiam furor iste tuus nos eludet? quem ad finem sese effrenata jactabit audacia?*" Certainly the presence of Mr. Calhoun in the Senate "abused their patience," for they held their seats under the Constitution, which they thought he meditated to overthrow; and his "unbridled audacity" in thrusting himself into a body, whose action, as a co-ordinate branch of the government, his measures threatened to destroy, excited their indignation.

Still, when with reverential manner, and in a serious, solemn, and audible voice he took the oath to support the CONSTITUTION OF THE UNITED STATES, opinion softened towards him; and many who had foreborne to accost him earlier now came forward, and with great sincerity, welcomed him to the Senate. He took all in good part; reciprocated the compliments he received, and concurred with others in the hope of harmonious legislation.

But all who had the fear or love of Gen. Jackson before their eyes, hated or professed to hate the southern chieftain. The thunders of the White House terrified as much in these days, as ever the thunders of the Vatican; no man would encounter them, unless for a purpose most safely and selfishly advantageous. The Jackson-men proper, were the most violent of the anti-Calhoun men. The Jackson press denounced him with less measured invective, than even his most prejudiced political opponents;—and the high-way to the old General's heart was supposed to be abuse of Mr. Calhoun.

But all moved him not; neither foreign defiance, "malice domestic," nor executive denunciation. The certainty of an overwhelming opposition to his cause, the clamor of an abusive press, the menace even of personal outrage—none frightened him from his propriety of word or action. He looked and bore himself "every inch" A MAN. They who disapproved most his theories or his acts, could not but admire his noble and undaunted bearing, or refuse him honesty of intention. His friends would have applied the eloquent language of the Roman poet to his conduct.

> "Justum et tenacem propositi virum,
> Non civium ardor prava jubentium
> *Non vultus instantis Tyranni*
> Mente quatit solida."

Mr. Calhoun, still new to his seat in the Senate, entered upon action in relation to the affairs of his State; a few days after his appearance, he introduced a resolution, calling upon the President for copies of his Proclamation of the 10th December, and Governor Hayne's counter-proclamation. These being communicated to the Senate on the 16th of January, Mr. Calhoun took the floor, and attacked with no little warmth of language the principles of the President's proclamation.

"The cry had been raised," he said, "that the Union was in danger. I know of no other danger than that of military despotism—I will proclaim it on this floor, that this is the greatest danger with which the Union is menaced—a danger the greatest which any country has to apprehend."

Mr. Forsyth rose to interrupt him. He said that on a motion to refer (Mr. Grundy having made a motion to that effect) all observations on the merits of the President's message were irrelevant and irregular.

Mr. Calhoun replied that he had so stated in the outset of his remarks, but, in the peculiar circumstances of his situation, had hoped and requested for a few minutes the indulgence of the Senate.

After the interchange of some explanatory remarks between these two gentlemen, the motion to refer was carried, and thereupon the Senate adjourned.

On Monday the 21st of January, Mr. Wilkins a Senator from Pennsylvania, introduced from the committee on the judiciary, of which he was chairman, a bill further to provide for the collection of duties on imports. This was the famous "Force Bill."

It seemed to partake somewhat of the character of the decree passed by the Senate of Rome, in political emergencies, "*videant consules, ne quid res publica detrimenti capiat*," the consuls should take care that the republic sustained no injury; investing them with powers unknown to peaceable times. It empowered the President to employ the naval or land forces, or militia of the United States to put down any armed or riotous assemblage of persons resisting the custom-house officers in the discharge of their duty, or in any manner opposing the execution of the revenue laws of the United States; limiting him to no expenditure of money for the purpose, but investing him,—the opponents of the bill contended,—with full and unquestionable power over the purse and sword. Mr. Poindexter, one of the most able as well as the most determined enemies to the measure, declared, that if the title of the bill corresponded to its provisions, it might be designated as "A bill to repeal the Constitution of the United States, and to vest in the President despotic powers."

Mr. Calhoun on the day succeeding, to repel the assault of the Executive as he considered this recommendation of the judiciary, brought forward in the Senate his celebrated resolutions, defining the powers of the general government, of which the most important was the following: "Resolved, That the people of the several States, thus united by the constitutional compact, in forming that instrument, and in creating a general government to carry into effect the objects for which it was formed, delegated to that government, for that purpose, certain definite powers, to be exercised jointly, reserving at the same time, each State to itself, the residuary mass of powers, to be exercised by its own separate government, and that whenever the general government assumes the exercise of powers not delegated by the compact, its acts are unauthorized, and are of no effect; and that the same government is not made the final judge of the powers delegated to it, since that could make its discretion, and not the Constitution, the measure of its powers; but that, as in all other cases of compact among sovereign parties, without any common judge, each has an equal right to judge for itself, as well of the infraction as of the mode and measure of redress."

He introduced these resolutions with some prefatory remarks, in terse, condensed, emphatic language—the beautiful structure of which, a word interpolated or withdrawn would deface if not destroy. The speech was not long—in duration, not more than half an hour; but it produced a greater impression than volumes of ordinary argument. It revealed to the friends of the administration the character of the enemy with whom they would be compelled to contend; it gave them to understand that in the conflict which was hastily approaching, there could be, on their part, no reserved strength; that all was to be exerted, and all, but with great dexterity and energy, in vain.

Mr. Grundy, the "next friend" to the President in the Senate, undertook the conduct of the bill through that body. Passing between the President and his principal adherents in the two Houses, he matured, in frequent consultation with both parties, his plan of operations. Canvassing the Senate, he found, among his political associates there, some unchangeably opposed to the principles and recommendations of the bill. Mangum and Brown of North Carolina, Poindexter of Mississippi, Tyler of Virginia, Bibb of Kentucky, all able debaters and hitherto most prominent of the Democratic party, threatened to oppose the passage of the bill, with all the strength of argument and skill in strategy they could command. Executive blandishments and executive menace availed naught against their purpose. They entrenched themselves within their State Rights' principles, as Wellington at Torres Vedras.

Nor among all not hostile to the bill was there great warmth of sentiment, or much promise of earnest co-operation, in its favor. Colonel Benton even, yielding to no one in devotion to the person and fortunes of the President, seemed to doubt the policy of dragooning a measure through the two Houses, upon the merits of which the party was so irreconcileably divided; an internecine war, he knew full well, would spring up between friends upon the issue, and rage with fiercer intensity than between hereditary or natural foes. He was at this time, besides, on terms of even intimacy with Mr. Calhoun, whose ingenuous character and transcendent ability he omitted no occasion to dwell upon in enthusiastic terms. He was reluctant to be brought into personal conflict with one, against whom he had no ground of individual complaint; but with whom, on the contrary, he entertained sentiments in regard to political action and theories, so nearly homogeneous. His vote was safe for the bill, but he was not prepared to take an active or leading part in securing its success.

Others promised votes and all the influence, personal and political, they could exert in support of the measure; some from a conviction of its necessity, and some from devotion to the party or to General Jackson—which they considered identical ideas.

But a numerical majority barely, though assured beyond a doubt, was not all the administration sought. To be successful in the vote, and yet worsted in the argument, would be a barren victory; a victory, more humiliating and even more fatal, than an honorable defeat. Before the great tribunal of PUBLIC OPINION, the cause was to be argued; and upon its decision, and not upon the votes of complying Congressmen, were the merits of the question, and the honesty, and ability, and future destiny of the actors to be determined. From such decision, there was no appeal; and the friends of the administration, nervously sensitive of the importance of the contest, determined to spare no exertion to gain a favorable verdict. It was, in truth, to them, a life-and-death struggle. Not even the overwhelming popularity of General Jackson conld long have upholden his administration against the stunning effects of hostile OPINION, on this momentous question.

Yet there were of the Democratic party in the Senate, who favored the bill, some of distinguished capacity, of whom was Rives of Virginia, deeply versed in Constitutional law; a logician of much astuteness, an earnest and fluent debater, and of a mind too liberal and too comprehensive, to be restricted to the contemplation solely of isolated abstractions; Dallas of Pennsylvania, whom forensic training and natural talent admirably qualified for controversial argument; Wilkins, also of Pennsylvania, less eminent than his colleague as a lawyer and statesman, but of no inferior parts; Forsyth of Georgia, possessing qualities of mind as extraordinary in their variety as their several excellence—a wit, ready and polished, that loved to play not wound—an imagination ardent but well regulated—a fancy, expressive, glowing, and chaste—a memory tenacious and reliable—and a judgment discriminating, profound and correct; GRUNDY himself, a persuasive speaker, of an imposing presence and conciliatory manner, an admirable tactitian withal, that understood and could regulate the springs of action.

But all the combination of such various talents, powerful as it was, the administration felt deeply would not avail against Mr. Calhoun. He was in himself equal to the whole strength the administration could put forth. He had all his antagonists had, and more; more vigor of thought and energy of expression, a greater variety and depth of acquisition, and more knowledge of the science of government; and, above all these, a power of analysis and combination, which could resolve the most complex ideas into their original elements, and, by the process of generalization, from materials thus reduced to his will, construct one harmonious system of lofty and impregnable truths. He had in fine, genius, while the rest had but talent, however eminent.

In this great crisis of the party and the country, Mr. Grundy felt that it was necessary to seek elsewhere than from his political associates. His eyes were turned where all other eyes were turned. There was but one man, the friends of the administration felt, who could rescue the government and the country from the dangers that encompassed and threatened to overwhelm them. And he of all men was the person they had sought most to injure.

From imperative engagements elsewhere, Mr. Webster had been but little time in the Senate during the earlier discussion of the bill, and had taken no part in it. His apparent indifference to its fate added to the apprehensions of the friends of the measure, made them still more anxious to gain his support. Democratic members of both houses hung round his friends, seeking by every argument, promise or entreaty their favorable influence with him—a member of General Jackson's cabinet came to him at his lodgings, and earnestly besought him to take the lead in defence of the measure—to assume the controlling management of it, and to suggest whatever amendments he deemed necessary. It was indeed full time for his appearance. The South Carolinian Hector was pursuing his enemies to their very last entrenchments, threatening to involve in one common ruin the administration, the Constitution and the country, while Achilles was absent from the battle.

Mr. Webster, like the hero of the Grecian epic, might have listened to his enemies and turned an unheeding ear to the supplications of his late assailants. He might have "fretted his great heart" in silence, safe in his haughty isolation, and left his enemies to perish.

But private griefs, nor any considerations of a private character ever controlled his regard for the public interest; the one has been with him at all times postponed to the other. In the present case, he held the cause of the administration, the cause of the constitution, and of the country—if the former went down on this issue, the constitution and the country would go down with it. He forgot, therefore, the contumelious treatment he had received, forgot the injuries done and intended him, and rallied his whole strength in support of the persons to whom, for the time, the interests of his country were intrusted.

CHAPTER X.

Mr. Wilkins of Pennsylvania, who introduced the bill, commenced the debate upon it. He opened the case for the government. His introductory remarks were well conceived and expressed, moderate in tone, and pertinent. He was not allowed to proceed, however, without interruption. Messrs. Calhoun and Miller of South Carolina, and Poindexter of Mississippi, broke in upon him with interrogatories, explanations, and denials, continually, during the first day of his speech. The second day he got along with less difficulty, though not uninterruptedly; Mr. Calhoun watching every word that fell from him, and gainsaying many. "The moment," said Mr. Wilkins, "we fail to counteract the nullification proceedings of South Carolina, the Union is dissolved; for, in this government of laws, union is obedience, and obedience is union. The moment South Carolina—

Mr. Calhoun, interposing—"Who relies upon force in this controversy? I have insisted upon it, that South Carolina relied altogether on civil process, and that, if the general government resorts to force, then only will South Carolina rely upon force. If force be introduced by either party, upon that party will fall the responsibility."

Mr. Wilkins—" The general government will not appeal, in the first instance, to force. It will appeal to the patriotism of South Carolina—to that magnanimity of which she boasts so much"—

Mr. Calhoun, with some asperity—"I am sorry that South Carolina cannot appeal to the sense of justice of the general government"—and hereupon, two or three Senators called him to order. So far from being considered laudable, it was holden censurable then for any Senator to speak in objurgatory terms of the general government. To have spoken of *the advantages* of separation or secession, would have provoked for the offender, the indignation or contemptuous pity of the House, in which such sentiments were proposed. Twenty years before this, in 1811, when a distinguished member from Massachusetts, in a debate on the bill for the admission of Louisiana, in the House of Representatives, used these expressions—" If this bill passes, the Union is virtually dissolved; and it will be the right of all, and the indispensable duty of some of the States, to prepare definitely for a separation—amicably, if they can, forcibly, if they must," the Speaker, Joseph B. Varnum, of Massachusetts, formerly a soldier of the Revolution, decided that it was not in order to use words in debate which threatened the stability of the Union. But parliamentary manners have changed since, and members of Congress now threaten disunion, not only without attracting censure, but even attention. The idea no less than the word seems to have become endurable.

Mr. Wilkins continued and concluded his speech the second day, when Mr. Bibb of Kentucky, took the floor. His appearance gave a character to his words. He retained somewhat of the old school in his manner and dress. His words, too, were selected and enunciated with great particularity. But though formal, his manner was not cold; nor was his language, though precise, without force. "I have witnessed," he said, in his exordium—"the ragings of the natural elements, when the blackening clouds gathered. I have seen the forked flashes blaze upon the mountain, and yet the rock that decked the mountain's brow, and defied the storm, remained unscathed by the lightnings of heaven. I have heard the clamoring of the winds, and seen the proud forest bend before the majesty of nature. In the fury of the storm, I have seen the fond mother press her infant to her bosom, and sigh, with fearful apprehension that her husband might be exposed, houseless, 'to bide the peltings of the pitiless storm.' But, in the darkest gloom of elemental strife, there was a consolation; for there was an assurance that the storm would cease; that the sun would again shed his gladdening rays, on herb, tree, fruit, and flower, displaying the charms of nature in renovated health and refreshened verdure. But when, in the storm now gathering in the political horizon, I shall hear the blast of a trumpet, the neighing of the steeds, the noisy drum, the resoundings of the heavy-toned, fiery-mouthed cannon; when I shall see the glittering of small arms; when I shall read the proclamation preparatory to mortal strife between State and State, and know that the strife is in fact begun 'in all the pride, and pomp, and circumstance of war,' I shall then despair. There will be no assurance that the Constitution will erect its proud crest above the struggling hosts, and come out unscathed from the contest. I have no assurance that the Union will survive the carnage and embittered feelings engendered in the impious war of child against parent, brother against brother." This, after all, seems a kind of speech that occupies the debateable ground between eloquence and bathos; a decided lurch either way would conclude its destiny. A man without ability could not use such language; a man of great abilities would not.

The whole of his first day, Mr. Bibb used for an historical introduction to his speech. He gave, in great detail, the proceedings of States antecedent to the adoption of the Constitution. The second day he devoted to a consideration of the powers of the general government under the Constitution; and, before the close of the senatorial day, he exhausted, if not the subject, his audience and himself.

He gave way about two o'clock in the afternoon to Mr. Poindexter, who moved an adjournment; but the Senate refused to adjourn. Wherefore Mr. Buckner of Missouri, moved to postpone the further consideration of the bill, and to make it the special order for the next day.

Mr. Webster rose to a point of order, The gentleman from

Kentucky had given way, in the usual manner, to a motion to adjourn. Such was the practice of the Senate. But if a gentleman yielded the floor for any other motion, he yielded the right to resume it.

Whereupon Mr. Poindexter rose, and said, with some warmth of manner—"It must be apparent to the Senate, that the question now before the Senate is one of the greatest importance. I have never before seen a disposition manifested by this body to refuse to a member an opportunity for rest and research, in order to enable himself to close his argument in a manner which would be satisfactory to himself and the country. If the Senator from Massachusetts is disposed to speak to the Senate for a week, I will always vote for adjournment when requested."

The Chair having decided that if a Senator yield the floor for any other motion than a motion to adjourn, he lost the right of the floor, Mr. Poindexter made another unsuccessful motion to adjourn.

Thereupon Mr. Bibb rallied, and spoke with accustomed fluency for a few minutes, when the Senate, giving way to a sense of weariness, consented to adjourn.

There are few men, of however eminent ability, who can command listening senates three entire days in succession, upon one subject. Our logomachies astound our trans-Atlantic cotemporaries, who cannot comprehend, from their own experience, our protracted debates. The discussion of a bill in the British Parliament occasionally outlasts a day's or night's session; an individual speech, never. The commencement and conclusion must be of one day; the unities being as strictly observed as in the Greek drama.

The experiment with us of long, tedious speeches is fatal to the ill-advised perpetrator. The attention wearies, the mind revolts, at such atrocious outrage against the fitness of things. He who talks much performs little.

Mr. Bibb's third day speech was listened to but from courtesy. He seemed himself finally to become affected by the atmosphere of dullness he had called around him, and hastened to a close. His speech evinced much judgment; and it was to be regretted no less for his sake than for others, that he had not exhibited more and spoken less.

Mr. Frelinghuysen of New Jersey appropriated all the remnant that was left of Mr. Bibb's third day, and a portion of the day following. His argument was respectable, not brilliant. "We rely," said he, "upon the peaceful energies of our institutions; Europe, on the thunder of her cannon and the clangor of her arms. Poor Holland is about to pay dearly for this balance of power. For two hundred years it has deluged Europe with blood. Here we have it in a peaceful tribunal, by which the tranquillity of the country and the safety of our institutions may be preserved for years to come. Just and certain retribution will come upon those who destroy this peaceful arbiter, and set up the sword in its stead. Here is the system, sir, as I understand it, as I honor it, and as I, with my latest breath, will maintain it. I regard this system as by far the greatest political blessing ever given by Providence to any people. To it I trace all our happiness and prosperity. In this day of our highest prosperity, when our fountains are all full, and our streams running over, do not let a sister State rashly overturn the institutions which are the sources of our happiness. How painful is the crisis which seeks disunion, and which would split us up into disgraced and bleeding fragments. This nullification, if it prevail, will yet meet a tremendous retribution, in the execrations of all future times." This is all proper, decent, and senatorial; it is also just to the character of its author, who gained as much influence in the Senate from his estimable moral qualities, as from his intellectual endowments.

Mr. Brown of North Carolina, followed Mr. Frelinghuysen, and took his stand, he said, on the reserved rights of States. "I repudiate the doctine of nullification. I repudiate also the high-toned doctrine of the Federal party. I believe it is to that high-toned doctrine that we are to attribute nullification." He contended that it was by an improper pressure of the federal government on the rights of the States, and by its exercise of doubtful powers, that South Carolina had been compelled to take the defiant position she had assumed; which, if not justifiable, was susceptible of great palliation. "Proud as I am"—he said in conclusion—"of the achievements which have been performed under the star-spangled banner; proud as I am of the stars and stripes which have fluttered in every sea and every clime; anxious as I am for the glory of the country; yet God forbid that these stars and stripes, which have been heretofore the rallying point of heroism, should now float over the mangled corses of our bleeding countrymen. God forbid that our country should undergo this sad and disastrous revolution; for he believed, whenever that should take place, not only the liberties of this country, but the best and brightest hopes of the civilized world, would be destroyed for ever."

Mr. Holmes, of Maine, then took the floor. Mr. Holmes would have been considered well qualified for the Senate, had he never been Senator; but what he gained in position, he lost in reputation. His bearing, manner, and speech, all wanted dignity. His wit, of which he had no inconsiderable portion, was coarse, and even vulgar; and his manner too often degenerated into buffoonery. But he had quickness of parts, and, what does not always accompany them, a retentive memory. If he did not originate much, he easily apprehended the merit of another's speech, and, from recollection and power of combination, was able to fashion one of his own. He was good, too, at repartee, and made himself formidable to those who feared his ridicule.

There was little he said in the course of his speech on this occasion worthy to be translated. As an example of his argumentative manner, the following passage may be given: "This is a Constitutional Government, and, therefore, it is sovereign as far as to all powers delegated to it. This is the general understanding of the people; and the idea of nullification and reserved rights is almost everywhere ridiculed by them. I saw a story in a Tennessee newspaper which I will relate, as apposite. A law of that State respecting marriage required the publication of the banns some time previous to marriage. The time appeared too long to one individual, and he determined to oppose the law and set himself down on his reserved rights. The law did not prohibit marriage, which would be flatly unconstitutional, but it delayed it, and was therefore injurious. He accordingly nullified the law."

The great merit of Mr. Holmes' argument on this occasion was its brevity; some of the other speeches wanted even that.

Mr. Tyler followed Mr. Holmes, on the opposite side of the question. "The pernicious doctrine," said he, "that this is a National and not a Federal Government, has received countenance from the late proclamation and message of the President. The People are regarded as one mass, and the States as constituting one nation. I desire to know when this chemical process occurred? When were the States welded together in one mass? Was it before or since the Revolution? At what time was Virginia fused into an integral mass with the other States?

* * * * * * *

This amalgamating doctrine is followed out into most singular consequences. Sir, it is said that I do not represent on this floor the State of Virginia, but the United States. Strange hallucination! This I must consider as vital in its consequences. It brings into question the great right of instructions;

for if it be true, the State of Delaware has as full and absolute control over my actions as the State of Virginia. No, sir, I repudiate this doctrine ; I owe no responsibility, politically speaking, elsewhere than to my State. And if any Senator from that State should dare oppose her instructions, I might say, with perfect confidence, to quote the remarks of one of her most gifted sons, that "if he would not be instructed in his seat, he would very soon be instructed out of it." The doctrine is founded in a gross misconception of the nature and character of our institutions."

This speech reflects the style and character of Mr. Tyler—the defects and merits alike of both. Occasionally, there will be found a fitful energy of expression and purpose, but close beside, an obscurity of phrase, and a seeming hesitation, that throw an air of insincerity upon the sentiments uttered. Great fluency of speech, to the frequent detriment of ideas—an overflowing of historical illustration, to the partial submersion of the subject-matter—forgetfulness of general interests in the intense contemplation of personal objects—arguments often without conclusion, and conduct often without motive—such seem to have been the distinguishing characteristics of Mr. Tyler's speech and public life.

His argument and course, on this eventful occasion, neither great in themselves, were the causes of great results. They revealed a half-formed inclination to secede from the embodied idea of Democracy ; an inclination that grew into a purpose, and thence into action, within a brief period, to such a developement, that the Whigs, a few years after, used his name as leaven, to produce fermentation among the State Rights' constituency of the South. The fermentation ensued, and the Whigs gained their less than Phyrrus-victory* of 1840.

"I would," said Mr. Tyler, in his peroration, "that I had but moral influence enough to save my country in this hour of peril. If I know myself, I would peril all, everything that I hold most dear, if I could be the means of stilling the agitated billows. I have no such power; I stand here, manacled in a minority, whose efforts can avail but little. You, who are the majority, have the destinies of the country in your hand. If war shall grow out of this measure, you alone are responsible. I will wash my hands of the business. Rather than give my aid, I would surrender my station here, for I aspire not to imitate the rash boy who sat fire to the Ephesian dome. No, sir, I will lend no aid to the passage of this bill. I had almost said that 'I had rather be a dog and bay the moon than such a Roman.' I will not yet despair. Rome had her Curtius; Sparta her Leonidas; and Athens her band of devoted patriots;—and shall it be said that the American Senate contains not one man who will step forward to rescue his country in this her moment of peril? Although that man may never wear an earthly crown, or sway an earthly sceptre, eternal fame shall wreathe an evergreen around his brow, and his name

* "Another such victory, and we are ruined," Phyrrus said, of his triumph over the Romans.

shall rank with those of the proudest patriots of the proudest climes."

Mr. Tyler makes a liberal use of Plutarch in his speech. There are, indeed, more Greeks and Romans in it than Americans. It is a fault (or virtue) common to his State.*

Mr. Clayton followed, and ably refuted, Mr. Tyler. In answer to Mr. Tyler's declaration that he was a Senator of Virginia, and not of the United States, Mr. Clayton said: "Sir, were it not for sheer compassion towards some of those gentlemen, who indulge us so often with extravagant declamation about State power and State supremacy, it would be well to ring the truth daily in their ears, until they are cured of these diseased imaginations, that neither the "Old Dominion," nor even the "Empire State" herself, could singly, and suc-

* Gen. Harrison was a native of Virginia and received his education there. To his last day, he never recovered from Plutarch. His Inaugural Message proves the duration of his attachment. Plutarch's heroes would have appeared therein in still greater number, but for an untimely fate that kept them out.

It was said at the time, that the morning before the Message was delivered, the Secretary of State elect was met, by a friend, walking in the vicinity of the White House, in no little apparent perturbation. "What is the matter with you, this morning, Mr. Webster?" inquired his friend; "you seem agitated." "Agitated, sir! and who would not feel agitated, that had committed the murder I have this morning?" "Murder! Mr. Webster?" "Aye, sir, murder; murder, with malice aforethought, *of I know not how many Greeks and Romans.*"

There is no authority, however, but rumor for this story.

cessfully, measure strength with one of the second-rate powers of Europe. The gentleman from Virginia, who has filled his present station with so much honor to himself and usefulness to his country, denies that he is a Senator of the United States, and asserts that he is only a Senator of Virginia. He denies the very existence of such a character as that of a Senator of the United States. Each member here, in his view, is bound to legislate for his own State, and can represent no other. But where is the clause in the Constitution which recognizes a Senator of Virginia, of Delaware, or of any other single State, in this hall? This is not the Senate of Virginia, but of the United States. The honorable member says he acts here only in obedience to the wishes of Virginia; that he yields obedience to this Government only because Virginia wills it. The Constitution and laws of the United States have no binding force with him from any other cause than this, that Virginia commands him to obey them. The result of all this doctrine is, that whenever Virginia wills it, he will violate this Constitution, and set these laws at defiance. In opposition to all this, hear the creed of a national republican: I obey this Constitution, and act as Senator of the United States under it, because I have sworn to support that Constitution. I hold myself bound, while acting in my station here, to legislate for the benefit of the whole country, not merely for that of any section of it; and, in the discharge of my duty, I will look abroad throughout this wide Republic, never sacrificing the interests of any one part of it merely to gratify another, but always dealing out and distributing equal justice to all my countrymen, wherever they may be located, or by whatever title they may be distinguished from each other."

The eloquent patriotism of these and kindred remarks gained Mr. Clayton deserved consideration, among all parties. The liberality of his views was no greater, in the meantime, than the force of his argument. Oftentimes, during his speech, he was interrupted by Mr. Calhoun, who sought to obviate the effect of his logic, by the interposition of ingenious objections.

On Mr. Clayton's conclusion, Mr. Mangum obtained the floor, and moved to postpone the farther consideration of the bill till the next day. He wished to speak upon the bill, but was too unwell this day.

The Senate, however, did not wish to postpone the discussion of the bill. The majority thought its immediate passage necessary. The threatening attitude of South Carolina was to be met by an immediate preparation on the part of the general government, for all emergencies. The President's particular friends in the Senate urged action. Forsyth, Grundy, and Wilkins contended that the debate should go on. Mr. Calhoun said that the Senator from North Carolina was the only member of the Committee on the Judiciary who had objected to the bill. He would appeal to the Senate, therefore, whether, on the score of justice, the gentleman was not entitled to such indulgence as he might require to enable him to give a satisfactory exposition of the reasons by which he was actuated, the more especially as he appeared so unwell.

Mr. Wilkins replied that he would be the last man to force the gentleman from North Carolina, for whom he had a great respect, into the discussion without mature preparation. But he thought the gentleman was fully prepared to debate the question at this time.

Mr. Calhoun said that the Senator from Pennsylvania could not have heard the Senator from North Carolina ask the postponement on account of his indisposition.

Mr. King, of Alabama, made the same suggestion; but Mr. Wilkins replied to neither.

Mr. Wilkins, in truth, displayed great eagerness to get the bill through; and some said at the time, from interested motives. "He votes for this great measure," said a Senator in this debate, "because it confers power on one, 'who never abused power.' He goes for the man, and sustains the principle for the sake of the man." He afterwards went for the mission to Russia, and got it; as the opponents of this bill contended, for his ready services on this occasion. But detraction is as inseparable from distinguished merit, as the shadow from the substance.

The intellectual sparring continued, and afforded relief to the graver discussion of the bill. Mr. Webster said there was no occasion for postponement. The bill could make progress, and the gentleman from North Carolina could be heard on any other day as well as this. But few days remained of the session, and if the bill was to be definitely acted upon, it could only be done by a determination to sit out the discussion. The Senate should sit till late in the evening, for at the rate of a speech a day, the bill would never be got through.

Mr. Calhoun replied, that if any other Senator, on either side of the house, was ready to go on with the debate, he would make no objection to sit out the day. But he thought the gentleman from North Carolina was, in justice, entitled to the indulgence of the Senate.

Mr. King said, that if the gentleman from Massachusetts wished to deliver his sentiments on the bill, he hoped the motion would be withdrawn for that purpose, and he would be happy to listen to the gentleman to as great length as he might desire.

Mr. Webster—"The gentleman from Alabama is extremely kind; and his kindness is justly appreciated. The gentleman from Massachusetts fully understands the gentleman from Alabama; but he has no disposition to address the Senate at present, nor, under existing circumstances, at any other time, on the subject of this bill."

The argument, thus far, Mr. Webster thought preponderated in favor of the bill. His aid, therefore, was not called for; and he reserved it till it should be needed. But the friends of the President, in the Senate, who watched every word and movement of friend and foe, were alarmed, fearing lukewarmness on his part; and some left their seats, and crossed over to consult with him.

The motion to postpone was lost; and Mr. Mangum took the floor on the bill. But after proceeding for fifteen minutes, or thereabouts, he yielded the floor to Mr. Poindexter, who moved that the Senate adjourn, as the gentleman from North Carolina was evidently too much indisposed to proceed. The Senate, however, refused to adjourn, and Mr. Mangum resumed his argument.

He drew a parallel between the course pursued by the British Government previous to the war of the Revolution, and that which was now pursued by the General Government against South Carolina; a parallel, however, that like parallel lines, might run on forever without meeting. After continuing in this strain for some time, Mr. Mangum again gave way to Mr. Sprague, of Maine, who moved an adjournment, which was lost by one vote.

Mr. Mangum recommenced his argument, and continued it till 4 o'clock, when Mr. Tyler, premising that the Senate had by this time sufficiently indicated its intention to sit till a late hour every afternoon, for the purpose of bringing the debate to a close, moved that the Senate adjourn.

Mr. Webster would not oppose the motion, but rose to give notice that, for one, he should vote hereafter against any motion to adjourn before six o'clock, till the bill was disposed of.

The main action of the drama was relieved by occasional episodes, as in the Grecian Epic, where, while the armies pause, valiant spirits on either side get up a single combat. Of such nature was the passage-at-arms between Grundy of Tennessee, and Poindexter of Mississippi, upon the subject of the military orders of the President. The most intense cu-

10

riosity and deepest silence prevailed in relation to the President's intentions of a forcible demonstration against South Carolina. It was currently reported that the General had ordered a portion of the fleet to occupy Charleston harbor, and had given instructions of a belligerent character to the commander of the military forces at and near Charleston. Poindexter, who affected to assume a certain kind of leadership in the debate against the bill, introduced a resolution, calling upon the President for information of his action or intentions. He had been an early Jackson-man, but had *ratted*, since his election to the Senate. He never was constant to a man or principle long. He embraced a friendship or measure with vehemence and gave them up with precipitancy. He hated cordially, and enjoyed the faculty, to a greater extent than almost any other man, of inspiring cordial hatred. All he aimed at seemed to be notoriety; or, if he sought it not, it came to him, gratuitously.

Partly to indulge this passion, and partly to exasperate Gen. Jackson—between whom and himself there raged a personal warfare, *bellum plusquam civile*, as Lucan has it—he threw this resolution into the Senate, and provoked a discussion with Mr. Grundy, against whom, as the nearest friend of the President, his remarks were mostly directed.

He said, that when the day before he introduced the resolution, he thought he had placed the gentleman from Tennessee in an awkward predicament, and now he was sure of it. The gentleman and his friends, after having consulted their pillows, had come to the Senate with a determination to destroy his resolution, if in their power to do so. He was sorry to see this opposition to his motion; it seemed to be indicative of a disposition to shroud in secrecy the movements of the Executive authority. "Sir," said he, "there was a drawing-room last night, and great anxiety was manifested on the part of some gentlemen, to get the ear of the President."

Mr. Grundy did not pretend to understand what the gentleman from Mississippi meant by his allusion to the drawing-room. He could approach the President as one of his constitutional advisers, and was not obliged to take advantage of the social character of the drawing-room, to reach his ear.

In regard to the information the Senator from Mississippi sought, he would suppose some most respectable citizens of South Carolina had communicated intelligence to the Executive, upon which secret orders had been issued; does the Senator ask the names of these citizens, and all the circumstances of their disclosures?

"All, all!" said Mr. Poindexter; "the whole of them."

"But would not such disclosure," asked Mr. Grundy, "lead to the immediate shedding of blood?"

"I care not if it does," replied Mr. Poindexter. "Let us have the information, no matter what are the consequences."

But Mr. Grundy was not disposed to gratify the truculent curiosity of the Senator from Mississippi, and after some good-natured bantering on his part, and the expression of some more indignation on the part of the Mississippian, the discussion was cut short by the action of the Senate, in taking up the special order of the day.

Of the nature of an episode, too, was the scene that occurred when Mr. Webster undertook to prove that the bill and the message of the President contained the same identical recommendations; and that, consequently, anathemas instead of being confined to the first, should be directed equally against the latter.

A warm controversy had risen on the measure, he said, and it was but proper to understand between what parties it existed.

Soon after the declaration of war by the United States against England, an American vessel fell in at sea with one of England, and gave information of the declaration. The English master inquired, with no little warmth of manner and expression, why the United States had gone to war with England? The American answered him, that difficulties had existed, for a good while, between the two Governments, and that it was at length thought, in America, to be high time for the parties to come to a better understanding.

"I incline to think, Mr. President," continued Mr. Webster, "that a war has broken out here, which is very likely, before it closes, to bring the parties to a better understanding. * * * Now, sir, let it be known, once for all, that this is an Administration measure; that it is the President's own measure; and I pray gentlemen to have the goodness, if they call it hard names, and talk boldly against its friends, not to overlook its source. Let them attack it, if they choose to attack it, in its origin."

Messrs. Tyler, Bibb, and Brown, of North Carolina, answered with some heat—the latter particularly—the suggestion that they hesitated to denounce the message, from fear of its author. Mr. Tyler said it was not the first time he had been placed in opposition to measures of which the President was the source, or of which the President approved. If the President has sent a Botany Bill, he would call it so, and as such oppose it. Mr. Bibb said, if the President desired that any such power should be given him, as the bill before them gave, he could find no expression of such desire in the message. He could not imagine that any President would have the daring effrontery to ask of Congress to give him such powers. Mr. Brown said, he had never looked to any quarter for instructions in regard to his vote on this bill, neither to the President nor Judiciary Committee—and he should not.

These interludes—if thus they may be called—added much to the interest of the main piece. They gave time, too, to the actors in the drama to better prepare their parts, to study their speeches, arrange their dresses, and—a thing not unattended to even by Senators—prepare good houses. For Senators, no more than professional actors, love not to appear to "empty boxes."

When the curtain again rose, in the regular piece, Mr. Dallas, of Pennsylvania, appeared, and spoke his speech "trippingly on the tongue." His personal appearance aided him no little. It was, punctually, that of a gentleman. His rubicund countenance, surmounted by hair white as the snow-flakes, bleached, but not thinned; his elaborate and improving manner, self-respecting yet not presumptuous; his scrupulous dress, subdued voice, and harmonious gesture, all bespoke the man of cultivated intellect and habits; and, in an assembly like the Senate of those days, could not fail to produce an earnest impression.

His language was consonant with his manner and bearing; it illustrated both. "Let us," said he, "inquire into the nature of our political structure. What is this political being—the Union, commonly styled 'the United States?' A consolidated multitude? Certainly not a federation merely of totally distinct masses of people? Certainly not. It is something then of a complicated character between these two, or combining them both. To be justly appreciated, it must be well understood, and not flimsily considered. Generalization and vague abstractions delude us, and necessarily lead to false conclusions. No one denies or doubts that the Constitution was formed by the people of the United States; and no one denies or doubts that it acts directly upon the people. Its origin and action are therefore popular or national. But was it not formed by the people as distinct aggregates called States in their sovereign capacities? Clearly it was. And is it not carried on, through some of its essential processes, by the separate States as sovereigns? Clearly it is. Its origin and action are then federative. Thus it is both popular and federative ; or, in other words, it is an entire national government, of which both the union and the distinctiveness of the sovereign States are fundamental and inherent qualities."

Mr. Miller, of South Carolina, followed Mr. Dallas, in a speech of some power, against the bill ; and Mr. Rives, of Virginia, followed Mr. Miller, in favor of the bill. It was Mr. Rives maiden speech, and a very creditable effort. He came out from the shadowy, spectral region of abstractions, where no life is visible, into the world of sense and action. There was a meaning and warmth in his language that gained sympathy and response in the breasts, no less than in the understandings, of his hearers. He nationalized Virginia, giving it more than " a *local* habitation and a name."

It was late in the evening of the fourteenth day of February, that Mr. Rives concluded his speech. On his resuming his seat, Mr. Calhoun said he had waited to see if any other member of the committee desired to speak on the bill. Wishing to be heard himself on its merits, he would move that the Senate adjourn—and the Senate adjourned.

CHAPTER XI

It was on the fifteenth day of February, 1833, that Mr. Calhoun addressed the Senate against the Force Bill. All were silent as he rose, and, intent upon every word he uttered, directed their eyes and ears towards him. There was no one in the country at the time whose every act was watched with so much care. He was, indeed, an object of fearful curiosity. What he meditated was unknown in those days, and may never be revealed. But the current and specious voice attributed to him no less than treason against the government, It was known he was ambitious; and, in the pursuit of his ambitious projects, it was believed he was unscrupulous. "What thou would'st highly, that would'st thou holily," was the confession by Lady Macbeth of her husband's character. But opinion at this time conceded no such doubtful compliment to Mr Calhoun. It was generally credited that no consideration of private or public morality, no restriction of personal or constitutional obligation, no recollections of the past, or fears of the future could control his mad ambition.

Prejudice amounted to a passion against him. The invectives hurled against him by General Jackson, and the accusations which followed them, in every multiplied form, rendered him an object of equal apprehension and hatred. He was denominated a Catiline by the organ of the administration, and by the people generally was feared as such.

The vulgar are disposed to confound moral with personal attributes; to judge of character or intention from physical developments; to believe what *seems* must be the logical and inevitable cause of what *is*. It is a conclusion, however, not confined to the vulgar, the illiterate, the uninformed—but shared, in a degree at least, by intelligent and observant men. Mr. Calhoun's appearance had answered well the preconceived idea of a conspirator. Tall, gaunt, and of a somewhat stoop in figure, with a brow full, well formed, but receding; hair, not reposing on the head, but starting from it like the Gorgon's; a countenance, expressive of unqualified intellect, the lines of which seemed deeply gullied by intense thought; an eye that watched everything and rèvealed nothing, ever inquisitive, restless, and penetrating; and a manner emphatic, yet restrained, determined but cautious; persons who knew not his antecedents nor his actual position, would have pointed him out as one that might meditate great and dangerous pursuits. To an audience, already embittered, he seemed to realize the full idea of a conspirator.

Yet the purity of his private life, his high integrity, and scorn of meanness in man or thing, gained him a warmth of personal regard that nearly overrode the indignation felt for his contemplated or suspected plans. Opinion, at times, hesitated between hatred and admiration; a turbulent condition of the mind not suited to a dispassionate view of the object of its contemplation, but calculated, nevertheless, to increase the interest and anxiety felt for it.

The isolation and even danger of his position were not injurious to the influence of his eloquence. Those who hated him most, and could feel no sympathy in his cause, yet pardoned those who felt. A great man struggling with adversity, was a spectacle the gods loved to contemplate, and which painters of every age have been always eager to express. There is in it so much of moral sublimity, so much of soul-subduing grandeur, so much of more than mere mortal magnanimity, that the heart is carried away, as by a kind of surprise. Our sympathies are too strong for our convictions.

Mr. Calhoun rose and addressed the Senate. "Mr. President, I know not which is most objectionable, the provisions of this bill, or the temper in which its adoption has been urged. If the extraordinary powers with which the bill proposes to clothe the Executive, to the utter prostration of the Constitution and the rights of the States, be calculated to impress our minds with alarm at the rapid progress of despotism in our country, the zeal with which every circumstance calculated to misrepresent or exaggerate the conduct of Carolina in the controversy is seized on, with a view to excite hostility against her, but too plainly indicates the deep decay of that brotherly feeling which once existed between these States, and to which we are indebted for our beautiful federal system."

A more ingenious, yet seemingly less studied exordium will scarcely be found recorded in parliamentary annals. The orator, in simple but artful words, transposes entirely the relations of parties; and, with an assurance that an auditor would not dare to suppose aught but conscious innocence could command, demands sympathy for himself and Carolina, as suffering wrong. The earnest manner of the speaker, the sincerity of his countenance and his voice, and his well-known candor avoided the suspicion of intended imposition on his part. It was evident to all that he sought to produce belief from what himself believed. He could not change facts, but he could interpret them. He was not an impostor but fanatic.

His whole argument assumes the innocence of South Carolina. Nothing could be more erroneous, he said, than that South Carolina claimed the right to violate any provision of the Constitution. Her object was not to resist laws made in pursuance of the Constitution, but those made without its authority, and which encroach on her reserved powers. She did not claim even the right of judging of the delegated powers, but of those that were reserved; and to resist the former when they encroach upon the latter.

He illustrated his position with infinite ability, and with great beauty of language. In truth, the curious felicity of his diction threw such a dazzling lustre upon his sentiments as to conceal their real character. Forms of beauty gained the senses, to the exclusion of sober reflection; just as the appearance of Helen, in her immortal loveliness, overcame the matured convictions of Priam's counsellors.

In an earlier part of this book, some allusion was made to Mr. Calhoun's warm advocacy of the *protective* Tariff of 1816, and of the speech he made on the passage of that measure. It is but fair to admit his explanation of his conduct on that occasion, as expressed in his speech at this time. His speech then, he said, was an impromptu. It was delivered at the request of a friend, when he had not previously the least intention of addressing the House. "He came to me," said Mr. Calhoun, "when I was sitting at my desk writing, and said that the House was falling into some confusion, accompanying it with a remark that I knew how difficult it was to rally so large a body when once broken on a tax-bill, as had been experienced during the late war. Having a higher opinion of my influence than it deserved, he requested me to say something to prevent the confusion. I replied that I was at a loss what to say; that I had been busily engaged on the currency, which was then in great confusion, and which, as I stated, had been particularly under my charge, as chairman. He repeated his request, and the speech which the Senator from Pennsylvania, Mr. Dallas, has complimented so highly was the result."

The bill of 1816 being a revenue bill was, of course, constitutional; in urging it, did he commit himself to that system of oppression since grown up, and which has for its object the enriching of one portion of the country at the expense of the other?

Mr. Calhoun contended that it was as a friend to the reserved powers of the States, Gen. Jackson was so warmly supported at the South in the canvass of 1828. His election was hailed as their security. But the very event on which they had built their hopes had been turned against them; and the very person to whom they had looked as a deliverer, and whom, under that impression, South Carolina had striven for so many years to elevate to power, had become the most powerful instrument in the hands of his and their bitterest opponents, to put down them and their cause.

"Scarcely had he been elected," said Mr. Calhoun, "when it became apparent, from the organization of his Cabinet, and other indications, that all our hopes of relief through him were blasted. *The admission of a single individual into the Cabinet*, under the circumstances which accompanied the admission, threw all into confusion. The mischievous influence over the President through which this individual was admitted into the Cabinet, soon became apparent. Instead of turning his eyes forward to the period of the payment of the public debt, which was then near at hand, and to the present dangerous political crisis, which was inevitable, unless averted by a timely and wise system of measures, the attention of the President was absorbed by mere party arrangements, *and circumstances too disreputable to be mentioned here*, except by the most distant allusion."

Few persons, among our public men, have been so careful to avoid personalities in debate as Mr. Calhoun. Notwithstanding the wrongs, fancied or real, he had suffered, or supposed himself to have suffered, from Mr. Van Buren, I recollect now no other occasion in which he made, in public debate, any hostile allusion to that gentleman, or indulged, indeed, in language of abuse towards any personal or political adversary. This, in a country and age where personal criminations and recriminations, if not defended on principle, are tolerated and even encouraged by general practice, is no ordinary praise.

Of the accusation against him in the President's Proclamation, that he had been governed in his late course by feelings of disappointed ambition, he spoke in terms more of sorrow than anger. It ill became the Chief Magistrate, he said, to make such a charge. His whole career refuted it. The doctrine which he now sustained he had advocated from the passage of the Act of 1828, "the bill of abominations." When that bill came from the other House to the Senate, the almost universal impression was, that its fate would depend upon his casting vote. It was known, as the bill then stood, that the Senate was nearly equally divided; and as it was a combined measure, originating with the politicians and manufacturers, and intended as much to bear upon the Presidential election as to protect manufacturers, it was believed that, as a stroke of political policy, its fate would be made to depend upon his vote, in order to defeat Gen. Jackson's election as well as his own. The friends of Gen. Jackson were alarmed, and he

(Mr. Calhoun) was earnestly entreated to leave the chair, in order to avoid the responsibility, under the plausible argument, that if the Senate should be equally divided, the bill would be lost without the aid of his casting vote. The reply to this entreaty was, that no consideration, personal to himself, could induce him to take such a course; that he considered the measure as of the most dangerous character, calculated to produce the most fearful crisis; that the payment of the public debt was just at hand, and that the great increase of revenue which it would pour into the treasury would accelerate the approach of that period; and that the country would be placed in the most trying of all situations, with an immense revenue, without the means of absorption upon any legitimate or constitutional object of appropriation, and would be compelled to submit to all the corrupting consequences of a large surplus, or to make a sudden reduction of the rates of duties, which would prove ruinous to the very interests which were then forcing the passage of the bill. Under these views he determined to remain in the chair, and, if the bill came to him, to give his casting vote against it, and, in so doing, to give his reasons at large; but, at the same time, he informed his friends that he would retire from the ticket, so that the election of Gen. Jackson might not be embarrassed by any act of his. "Sir," said Mr. Calhoun, "I was amazed at the folly and infatuation of that period. So completely was Congress absorbed in the game of ambition and avarice, from the double impulse of the manufacturers and politicans, that none but a few appeared to anticipate the present crisis at which now all are alarmed, but which is the inevitable result of what was then done." As to himself, he had clearly foreseen what had since followed. The road of ambition lay open before him; he had but to follow the corrupt tendency of the times, but he had chosen to tread the rugged path of duty.

The character of this extraordinary man has been the theme alike of extravagant praise and obloquy, as zealous friendship or earnest enmity have held the pen. His sun has lately sunk below the horizon; it went down in all the splendor of noon-tide, and the effulgence of its setting yet dazzles the mind too much, to justify an impartial opinion. But whatever may be the diversity of opinion as regards his patriotism, or the integrity of his purpose, no one who respects himself will deny him the possession of rare intellectual faculties; of a mind capacious and enlightened; of powers of reasoning almost miraculous; of unequalled prescience; and of a judgment, when unwarped by prejudice, most express and admirable.

On this, the greatest occasion of his intellectual and political life, he bore himself proudly and gloriously. He appeared to hold victory at his command, and yet determined, withal, to show that he deserved it. There was a strength in his argument that seemed the exhaustion of thought, and a frequency of nervous diction most appropriate for its expression. The extreme mobility of his mind was felt everywhere and immediate. It passed from declamation to invective, and from invective to argument, rapidly, but not confusedly, exciting and filling the imagination of all.

In his tempestuous eloquence, he tore to pieces the arguments of his opponents, as the hurricane rends the sails. Nothing withstood the ardor of his mind ; no sophistry, however ingenious, puzzled him ; no rhetorical ruse escaped his detection. He overthrew logic that seemed impregnable, and demolished the most compact theory, in a breath.

No little portion of the speech was directed to the consideration of the philosophy of government, and the history of free institutions,—subjects which the orator had studied to complete mastery, and was amply capable to illustrate. He defended himself against the charge of "metaphysical reasoning." As he understood the proper use of the term, it meant the power of analysis and combination. "It is the power," he said, "which raises man above the brute ; which distinguishes his faculties from mere sagacity, which he holds in common with inferior animals. It is this power which has raised the astronomer from being a mere gazer at the stars to the high, intellectual eminence of a Newton or La Place, and astronomy itself, from a mere observation of insulated facts, into that noble science which displays to our admiration the system of the Universe. And shall this high power of the mind, which has effected such wonders when directed to the laws which control the material world, be forever prohibited, under a senseless cry of metaphysics, from being applied to the mighty purpose of political science and legislation ? I hold them to be subject to laws as fixed as matter itself, and to be as fit a subject for the application of the highest intellectual power. Denunciation may indeed fall upon the philosophical inquirer into these first principles as it did upon Galileo and Bacon, when they first unfolded the great discoveries which have immortalized their names; but the time will come when truth will prevail in spite of prejudice and denunciation, and when politics and legislation will be considered as much a science as astronomy and chemistry."

The crowd was great in the Senate chamber during Mr. Calhoun's speech; in the galleries more particularly. While he was uttering some of his brilliant periods, in the very torrent, tempest, and whirlwind of his eloquence, a man in the gallery suddenly confounded the audience by exclaiming, in a shriek-like voice, "Mr. President!" and before the presiding officer could take measures to repress the outrage, he continued, "Mr. President, something must be done, or I shall be squeezed to death!" It was sometime before order could be restored, or the dignity of the Senate re-established. The ludicrous nature of the interruption affected the gravity of almost every person present, even of grave Senators; of all, perhaps, but the orator, upon whose countenance there passed not the shade of an emotion. The rigid muscles showed no relaxation, but every feature remained unmoved and inflexible. He proceeded as if naught had occurred of singularity, and his deep and earnest tones soon recalled the minds of the audience to the subject they had for a moment forgotten.

He spoke parts of two days—concluding at two o'clock of the second day, as soon as he finished his speech, Mr. Webster took the floor in reply ; universal opinion assuming that he alone was qualified to follow Mr. Calhoun.

Before Mr. Webster consented to address the Senate on the bill, he had demanded the incorporation into it of certain amendatory provisions. Everything he asked was conceded by its friends. He prepared, therefore, or redrafted several of the most useful sections of the bill ; not those which looked to the application of military force, but such as provided for the full exercise of the judicial power of the United States, notwithstanding the State laws which had been passed to defeat the exercise of that jurisdiction.

The high and equal rank of these two rivals,—the greatest intellects, it is not invidious to say, of the whole country,—and the momentous nature of the contest between them drew, of course, a much greater than ordinary crowd to the Capitol. Mr. Webster's reply to Hayne had made curiosity more eager to hear him again ; while the singular position of Mr. Calhoun, the doubt of his purposes, and his unrivalled abilities, served equally to attract multitudes.

The Executive Department of the Government was represented daily in the Senate during the discussion of this measure by one or more of its members. The Chief Magistrate, it is true, conceded to precedence, and withheld his presence from the open debate. But members of his Cabinet gratified their own curiosity and his wishes, and appeared among the audience; no one of whom watched the proceedings and the various speeches with more anxiety than the Secretary of War, LEWIS CASS. He occupied a somewhat hazardous position. An aspirant after greater honors, he saw no certain way to preserve the present and secure the future. On the one side the fatal anger of Gen. Jackson threatened to pursue the slightest defection from his will; on the other, outraged State Rights would seek plenary vengeance against the person who wantonly or weakly assailed them. The first intimidated him with the loss of present position; the latter, with the loss of future pre-eminence. The organ through which the intentions of the President, if hostile to the pretended rights of States, must yet find expression in voice and act, the Secretary of War felt, that any measure of force, whether aggressive or merely defensive, would excite against his name great obloquy at the South. From a due regard to his own interests, therefore, as well as, undoubtedly, from a warm attachment to the Union, he labored with great earnestness to harmonize the conflicting elements; in which laudable endeavor, he was zealously seconded, generally, by the rest of the Cabinet.

After Mr. Webster's reply to Col. Hayne, in which the general opinion at the time held that the latter was worsted, Mr. Calhoun, in conversation with a friend, attributed the result to Mr. Hayne's want of previous training, and of proper constitutional knowledge; and intimated that with another competitor, Mr. Webster might not have borne off the honors of the contest so easily. That Mr. Calhoun was superior to Mr. Hayne, alike in natural capacity and acquired knowledge, will be generally and readily conceded; but that he obtained over Mr. Webster, in the dialectic contest now commemorated, more of a victory than Col. Hayne, there would be many to dispute. It needs a poet, it is said, to judge of poetry, and, reasoning upon the same principle, a constitutional lawyer alone could safely pronounce upon the merits of a constitutional argument. To estimate with nicety the relative ability of such profound arguments as those of Mr. Calhoun and Mr. Webster, must presuppose the power of making an equal one. Still, if the common judgment may be holden as arbiter—and to what more certain or more accurate have we to look—there would be no hesitation in the adjustment of the relative merits of the two efforts.

Mr. Webster, in his speech, confined himself closely to the argument. Unlike Mr. Calhoun, he indulged neither in personal explanations nor philosophical observations, which, however profound and brilliant in themselves, had no pertinency to the issue.

His statement of Mr. Calhoun's theory sounds like its refutation. "Beginning," he said, "with the original error, that the Constitution of the United States is nothing but a compact between sovereign States; asserting, in the next step, that each State has a right to be its own sole judge of the extent of its own obligations, and, consequently, of the constitutionality of laws of Congress; and, in the next, that it may oppose whatever it sees fit to declare unconstitutional, and that it decides for itself on the mode and measure of redress, the argument arrives at once at the conclusion, that what a State dissents from, it may nullify; what it opposes, it may oppose by force; what it decides for itself, it may execute by its own power; and that, in short, it is itself supreme over the legislation of Congress, and supreme over the decisions of the national judicature—supreme over the Constitution of the country—supreme over the supreme law of the land. However it seeks to protect itself against these plain inferences, by saying that an unconstitutional law is no law, and that it only opposes such laws as are unconstitutional, yet this does not, in the slightest degree, vary the result, since it insists on deciding this question for itself; and, in opposition to reason and argument, in opposition to practice and experience, in opposition to the judgment of others having an equal right to judge, it says only: 'Such is my opinion, and my opinion shall be my law, and I will support it by my own strong hand. I denounce the law. I declare it unconstitutional; that is enough; it shall not be executed. Men in arms are ready to resist its execution. An attempt to enforce it shall cover the land with blood. Elsewhere, it may be binding; but here, it is trampled under foot.' This, sir, is practical nullification."

Against all such theories, opinions, or heresies, Mr. Webster maintained,—

I. That the Constitution of the United States is not a league, confederacy, or compact, between the people of the several States in their sovereign capacities ; but a Government proper, founded on the adoption of the people, and creating direct relations between itself and individuals.

II. That no State authority has power to dissolve those relations ; that nothing can dissolve them but revolution ; and that, consequently, there can be no such thing as secession without revolution.

III. That there is a supreme law, consisting of the Constitution of the United States, acts of Congress passed in pursuance of it, and treaties ; and that, in cases not capable of assuming the character of a suit in law or equity, Congress must judge of, and finally interpret, this supreme law, so often as it has occasion to pass acts of legislation ; and, in cases capable of assuming, and actually assuming, the character of a suit, the Supreme Court of the United States is the final interpreter.

IV. That an attempt by a State to abrogate, annul, or nullify an Act of Congress, or to arrest its operation within her limits, on the ground that, in her opinion, such law is unconstitutional, is a direct usurpation on the just powers of the General Government, and on the equal rights of other States ; a plain violation of the Constitution, and a proceeding essentially revolutionary in its character and tendency.

These four propositions Mr. Webster maintained with a variety of illustration and power of argument that surprised even those who estimated his abilities most highly. The occasion certainly demanded all the intellect with which he had been endowed. His opponent had given to his argument such an air of plausibility as to deceive many. If he had not succeeded wholly in making the worse appear the better reason, he had staggered former convictions, and unsettled the most deliberate belief. All objections to his theory he had refuted and exposed to ridicule, and no one of his opponents had been able to recover from his vigorous and well-directed blows.

Within the scope of this work, it would be impossible to adduce sufficient of Mr. Webster's argument to justify a belief in his positions; a circumstance, the less to be regretted, perhaps, since to the general reader his propositions will appear self-evident truths. Still, no one in pursuit of examples of the most masterly logic; no one who seeks to acquire a certain knowledge of the theory and practice of CONSTITUTIONAL LAW; no one, in fine, who would behold the dignity of human reason in its loftiest expression, can safely pretermit the perusal and study of this great effort.

There was not the opportunity in this speech, as in the reply to Hayne, for the exhibition of the various powers of the speaker. Here no sarcasm was required, no humor, no wit, and no impassioned eloquence. The mind was to be convinced, not the passions excited. The effect was to be permanent, rather than immediate; and it was the cause of his country, not personal gratification, that the orator was to strive to establish.

In the earlier part of his speech, Mr. Webster made an allusion to his reply to Hayne. "Mr. President," he said, "if I considered the constitutional question now before us as doubtful as it is important, and if I supposed this decision, either in the Senate or by the country, was likely to be influenced in any degree by the manner in which I might now discuss it, this would be to me a moment of deep solicitude. Such a moment has once existed. There has been a time, when, rising in this place, on the same question, I felt, I must confess, that something for good or evil to the Constitution of the country might depend on an effort of mine. But circumstances are changed. Since that day, sir, the public opinion has become awakened to this great question; it has grasped it; it has reasoned upon it, as becomes an intelligent and patriotic community; and has settled it, or now seems in the progress of settling it, by an authority which none can disobey —the authority of the people themselves."

Still it was well, that Mr. Webster put forth unreserved the energies of his mind on this occasion. Nullification had in part recovered from the severity of his first blow, and, fostered by Mr. Calhoun, was again rearing its horrid front against the Union. It might have been successful, but for Mr. Webster's gigantic argument, in *theory*; it may be successful hereafter, but can only be so, since such argument, by *force*— No reason but *ultima ratio regum*—"the last reason of kings" or republics—can justify it now.

The words of solemn warning with which he concluded his argument, cannot be too often heard and repeated; and could not be more fitly introduced than now, when the idea of disunion seems once more to occupy the weak imagination of fanatics, at either extremity of the Union. "Mr.President, if the friends of nullification should be able to propagate their opinions, and give them practical effect, they would, in my judgment, prove themselves the most skilful architects of ruin, the most effectual extinguishers of high-raised expectation, the greatest blasters of human hopes, which any age has produced. They would stand up to proclaim, in tones which would pierce the ears of half the human race, that the last great experiment of representative government had failed. They would send forth sounds, at the hearing of which, the doctrine of the divine right of kings would feel, even in its grave, a returning sensation of vitality and resuscitation. Millions of eyes, of those who now feed their inherent love of liberty on the success of the American example, would turn away from beholding our dismemberment, and find no place on earth whereon to rest their gratified sight. Amidst the incantations and orgies of nullification, secession, disunion, and revolution, would be celebrated the funereal rites of constitutional and republican liberty."

The thronged Senate-chamber, while it listened to the deep tones of the speaker, as in his most impressive manner he pronounced this eloquent admonition, surged like the sea. You saw the undulating motion of the crowd, leaning forward to catch each word as it fell, and forced back to its original position. It was late in the evening when the orator got through his speech. The emotions of the multitude, which had been repressed during the day did not hesitate to find articulate and forcible expression under the protecting shadows of night; and hardly had the speaker concluded his remarks, before the galleries, rising to a man, gave a hearty, vociferous cheer, for "Daniel Webster, the defender of the Constitution."

Mr. Poindexter immediately started to his feet and moved an adjournment. But the presiding officer ordered the galleries to be cleared, refusing to put the motion to adjourn till after order had been restored; and then the Senate adjourned.

CHAPTER XII.

The debate languished after the conclusion of Mr. Calhoun's and Mr. Webster's speeches. The crowd that had filled the Senate Chamber daily to hear them, gradually thinned. The public curiosity to listen to the debate, which had grown stronger from its first opening to the GREAT ARGUMENT, reached its highest point at the conclusion thereof, and thence subsided into its ordinary character of indifference. There were some good speeches on the subject, however, made later. Mr. Forsyth made an able argument for the bill, and refuted, with brief but emphatic logic, the objections urged against it. He had not prepared himself fully for the discussion, but he spoke enough to convince his audience of his ability to say more, equally well. Mr. Miller, of South Carolina, followed him on the other side, as briefly if not as ably. Speaking of Mr. Webster's position towards the administration as compared with his position in the Hayne controversy, he said: "The Senator from Massachusetts is now the alpha with the powers that be; it is not long since he was the omega." Mr. Poindexter also made a speech. How much or little of other merit it possessed, it wanted one sadly—the merit of brevity. There was but little in his constitutional argument not better expressed by Mr. Calhoun or Mr. Tyler: in personal invective, however, he borrowed from neither of those gentlemen. He drew his inspiration therein from his disposition. Mr. Grundy spoke with a good deal of plausibility and ingenuity of argument, particularly against the assumed right of any State to secede from the Union, at its option. Mr. Ewing of Ohio followed, and closed the debate. He rose to speak about six o'clock in the evening, spoke half an hour, and then gave way to a motion for adjournment. The motion was lost. It was the determination of the managers of the bill to take a vote upon it before adjournment. Against such intention, Mr. Calhoun protested. He said that as the debate was closed on the part of the opponents of the bill, and as there was no disposition on their part to delay its passage, he hoped that the gentlemen on the other side would consent to postpone the final question until the morning, as the Senate was thin, and a bill of such importance ought to pass in a full Senate. Several gentlemen, he said, had retired from indisposition.

Mr. Wilkins rendered a tribute to the liberality of the gentleman from South Carolina, who had postponed his intention of addressing the Senate, and had thus facilitated the termination of the debate. But as the Senate had been notified that the bill would be urged through this evening, and as it was therefore to be presumed that every Senator was prepared to vote, and as the public mind was desirous that this question should be disposed of, he could not consent to delay.

Mr. Calhoun then moved that the Senate adjourn, but, after some interlocution with members near him, withdrew the motion.

Mr. Ewing then resumed, and continued his remarks till half-past nine o'clock, when he yielded the floor to Mr Holmes, who moved an adjournment.

By this time, Senators exhibited conclusive indications of exhaustion. Some nodded in their seats; others were strown upon the sofas behind the bar; a few had left the Senate, and gone to their lodgings. There were none who felt not fatigued, and almost overborne by the protracted and ardent contest. But the confidential friends of the President, Messrs. Wilkins and Grundy, would listen to no entreaty for adjournment. This was the day, this the hour, to determine the fate of the bill. Senators had suffered, perhaps, but they could suffer a little more, for their country. Their merit would be the greater from their present sacrifice.

Mr. Wilkins demanded the yeas and nays on Mr. Holmes' motion to adjourn; which, being taken, stood, thirteen for adjournment, twenty-three against it.

Mr. Ewing again took the floor, and spoke an hour longer.

In the meanwhile, several Senators, some favorable and some adverse to the bill, left the Senate, unwilling or unable to await the termination of the debate; the two Senators from Missouri among others, thereby avoiding a record of their vote.

As soon as Mr. Ewing concluded his speech, Mr. Webster demanded the ayes and noes on the passage of the bill. Whereupon Mr. Tyler rose, and moved that the Senate adjourn. He stated that he had been induced to make the motion because he saw that several Senators who were opposed to the bill were absent from their seats, and he thought that the bill had better receive its final action early in the morning.

Mr. Wilkins replied that the gentlemen whose seats were empty, had but a few minutes before withdrawn from the Senate, and he presumed that, as they must be in the immediate vicinity, they would return in time to vote on the bill.

The motion to adjourn was then lost by the decisive vote of twenty-seven noes to five ayes.

Mr. Calhoun and some of his friends, who had waited in or near the Senate till the last hope of delaying action on the bill was lost, now, with some parade, left the Senate and the Capitol, having first endeavored to persuade Mr. Tyler to accompany them. He replied, he would remain to the crack of doom, but he would record his vote against this tyrannical measure—though his vote should be the only one against it.

Finally, all efforts to postpone a vote having failed, the question on the passage of the bill was taken at half-past eleven o'clock, and decided as follows:

Yeas.—Bell, Chambers, Clayton, Dallas, Dickerson, Dudley, Ewing, Foot, Forsyth, Frelinghuysen, Grundy, Hendricks, Hill, Holmes, Johnston, Kane, Knight, Nandain, Prentiss, Rives, Robbins, Robbinson, Ruggles, Silsbee, Sprague, Tipton,

Tomlinson, Waggaman, Webster, White, Wilkins, Wright.—32.

Nay.—John Tyler.

And the Senate adjourned at midnight.

In this list will be found the great name neither of Benton, Clay, nor Calhoun. It is not known that Mr. Benton ever assigned a reason for not voting; but those who are acquainted with the public and private career of the distinguished Senator, can well believe that it was from no want of moral courage that he did not record his name. Mr. Clay stated to the Senate, the day after the vote, that he found it impossible to breathe the impure air of the Senate-chamber after dinner. He had been twice compelled to absent himself from the Senate in the evening; and the night before, he was prevented from giving the vote which he would have given with pleasure in favor of the bill which had then passed. Mr. Calhoun said, that he had been anxious the night before, the vote should be postponed till to-day, that it might be taken in the full Senate. With this object in view, he had then moved an adjournment, but the majority of the Senate was inexorable. The only course that then remained for himself and his friends was, to vote in a minority which would not contain the strength of the opposition to the bill, or to leave the Senate; and they had determined on the latter as the most correct course, and as the best calculated to convey an accurate expression of the feeling of the Senate.

Mr. Clay made no speech upon the bill. There may be

those who think his silence distinguished him more than his participation in the debate could have done; as the image of Brutus omitted in the pageant of the conqueror, was considered more honorable to him than its presence could have been. And there may be those who think that it indicated faint-heartedness, or lukewarmness at least, to have been so passive when such momentous interests were in discussion. Leaving such persons, if there be such, to the enjoyment of their various opinion, it may be well to suggest the probable solution of his taciturnity. It is well known that during the whole discussion, the eminent Senator was devoted, with an incessant and intense application, to the maturing and bringing forward of his COMPROMISE—a measure which, from its importance, of principle no less than detail, demanded the entire absorption of even his intellectual energies. This measure he succeeded to introduce before the passage of the Force Bill. Its healing character doubtless tempered the acrimony of debate upon that bill, and avoided any disastrous results from its passage. Many will contend that the principle and policy of this famous COMPROMISE were alike wrong, but none will deny to its distinguished author a magnanimous intention, nor to the measure itself a conciliatory result. It afforded to both of the two distinguished parties to this fierce controversy the opportunity of withdrawal, without personal dishonor or civil war—an opportunity neither was reluctant to embrace.

General Jackson took an early opportunity to express in

person to Mr. Webster, his sincere gratitude for the eminent services rendered by that gentleman, in such perilous moment, to his administration; and Mr. Livingston, the Secretary of State, repeatedly, and in warm terms, made his own acknowledgments besides. In truth, it was conceded everywhere that, but for the efforts of Mr. Webster, and of the friends who rallied under him, the administration would have fallen into a powerless and pitiable condition; an object of opprobrium to its friends, and of safe insult to its foes.

A community of sentiment and action, in this fearful crisis of our national history, brought General Jackson and Mr. Webster into stricter intimacy, social and political, than had previously ever subsisted between them. Some of the General's friends hoped, and more feared, a closer official relationship. In May of this year, Mr. Webster journeyed West; returning in June, he met Mr. Livingston in New York, then preparing to depart on his mission to France. It was understood at this time, in private and confidential circles, that, before leaving Washington, Mr. Livingston had had frequent and earnest conversations with General Jackson in relation to Mr. Webster's position; and that he had urged upon him the absolute necessity of securing Mr. Webster's continued support of his administration. To his suggestions General Jackson gave a favorable ear and acquiescence; and authorized Mr. Livingston to approach Mr. Webster upon the subject. These conversations and their result, Mr. Livingston, in his interview with him in New York, communicated to Mr. Webster.

That a seat in the cabinet was at the same time proposed to Mr. Webster, on the part of the President, through the same medium of communication, was a belief warmly entertained by some of the nearest friends of both parties. *One* fact it is allowable to mention; a distinguished Senator, a political and personal friend of General Jackson, brought Mr. Webster a list of the intended nominees for offices in the Eastern States, and asked him to erase therefrom the names of any, personally objectionable to him. This Mr. Webster declined to do, not wishing to place himself under any obligations to the administration, that might qualify the freedom of his action, either in support or repudiation of its measures.

On many points of what was then the proposed policy of the administration, there was no marked difference of opinion between these two eminent men; in its foreign policy, particularly, they almost entirely concurred; but there was a radical and fatal difference on the great question of the currency. The measures General Jackson thought it necessary to take to prevent pecuniary loss to to the country from the unchecked operations of the United States Bank, did not meet Mr. Webster's concurrence. Indeed, the removal of the government deposits from that institution, however justifiable on the ground of expediency or even necessity, was a measure of such formidable energy, as to confound some of the general's longest tried and not most timid supporters. It encountered Mr. Webster's opposition, and even denunciation. And this honest difference of opinion, in regard to a matter of temporary importance, prevented the union of the two master-spirits of the age, and blasted the patriotic hopes of the country.

How much of party animosity might have been assuaged, how much of public good promoted, and national honor how greatly advanced, by the consummation of such an union ! How high the tide of public prosperity had risen, with such luminaries in conjunction !

The moral and intellectual attributes of one were the complement of the other. Not that both did not possess mental and moral characteristics of the same nature ; but some one quality would appear more predominant in one, and some other quality, equally distinguished, in the other ; both more brilliant from contrast.

History records few instances of more adamantine will and inflexibility of purpose, than characterized Andrew Jackson. Napoleon himself had not greater, nor more intuitive knowledge of men, or far-reaching sagacity. What he willed he accomplished ; his mind never faltered, and his purpose never changed.

He was got up on the statuesque model of a hero of Plutarch. His qualities were all clearly and boldly defined ; but without extravagance or deformity. There was nothing common-place in his character or thought. He acted and spoke with the freshness and power of genius. He dared everything ; yet to his dauntless nature there was added a haughtiness of spirit that withheld him from vulgar strife. He rushed to his purpose like a torrent from the mountain; no obstacle could retard his course, nor opposition restrain his impetuosity. The fiery vehemence of his will swept everything before it. Men gazed at its resistless career, and gave way, overcome with apprehension. To oppose him was to encounter destiny.

Such a determined will and fearless nature, with attendant power, wanted but direction to accomplish miracles of good. Such direction could have been found in Mr. Webster, whose comprehensiveness of view, calmness of deliberation, sagacity, and singleness of purpose had admirably qualified him for a controlling adviser. His intellectual majesty would have secured the admiration of his great ally, and tempered the vehemence of his action. He would have had the mind to plan what the other would have had the heart to execute. He would have been the engineer to give direction and speed to the locomotive; regulating its power, according to the obstacles to be overcome, or the thing to be accomplished.

But no such happiness was reserved for the country. A strong schism supervened within a year after Mr. Webster's defence of the administration, between him and the President; and the country went on in a career of intermittent disaster.

After the adjournment of Congress in the spring of this year (1833,) Mr. Webster visited the West. No conqueror flushed with recent victories could have had a more triumphal reception. His progress was one ovation. Cities poured out their crowds on his approach, tendering hospitality; and municipal authorities entertained him while he tarried. Invitations soliciting a visit were sent to him from every State of the West, expressed in warm and urgent language. At Buffalo, a public dinner and other courtesies were extended to him. His brief visit compelled him to decline the dinner; but he addressed the citizens of the place, and was responded to with enthusiasm. At Pittsburgh, in Pennsylvania, he was received with even more marked distinction. The citizens turned out *en masse*, and waited for his arrival at a spacious grove, where a handsome entertainment was prepared for him. The mayor of the city, in presenting him to the crowd, addressed to them these, among other words: "Gentlemen, we are this day citizens of the *United* States. The Union is safe. Not a star has fallen from that proud banner around which our affections have so long rallied. And when, with this delightful assurance, we cast our eyes back upon the eventful history of the last year—when we recall the gloomy apprehensions, and perhaps hopeless despondency, which came over us, who, gentlemen, can learn, without a glow of enthusiasm, that the great champion of the Constitution—that DANIEL WEBSTER, is now in the midst of us. To his mighty intellect, the nation, with one voice, confided its cause of life or death. Ours is a government not of force, but of opinion. The *reason* of the people must be satisfied before a call to arms This consideration is it that imparts to intellectual pre-eminence in the service of truth its incalculable value. And hence the preciousness of that admirable and unanswerable exposition, which has put down, once and forever, the artful sophisms of nullification."

In reply, Mr. Webster said, in allusion to General Jackson's conduct during the perilous crisis of nullification: "Gentlemen, the President of the United States was, as it seemed to me, at this eventful crisis, true to his duty. He comprehended and understood the case, and met it as it was proper to meet it. While I am as willing as others to admit that the President has, on other occasions, rendered important services to the country, and especially on that occasion which has given him so much military renown, I yet think the ability and decision with which he resisted the disorganizing doctrines of nullification, created a claim, than which he has none higher, to the gratitude of the country, and the respect of posterity. The issuing of the proclamation of the 10th of December, inspired me, I confess, with new hopes for the duration of the Republic. I would not be understood to speak of particular clauses and phrases in the proclamation: but its great and leading doctrines, I regard as the true and only true doctrines of the Constitution. They constitute the sole ground on which dismemberment can be resisted. Nothing else, in my opinion, can hold us together. While those opinions are entertained, the Union will last; when they shall be generally rejected and abandoned, that Union will be at the mercy of a temporary majority in any one of the States."

At other places which he visited he was received with no less consideration. His engagements at home prevented him from accepting the greater part of the invitations extended him, and compelled him, reluctantly, to return.

All this was the grateful response of the people to a meritorious servant. It was the expression of their opinion of the value and extent of his services—the voluntary homage of their heart. These, however, were not the first testimonials of public gratitude for great constitutional services Mr. Webster had received. For his previous effort in defence of the Constitution, he had been honored with the grateful thanks of some of the wisest and best men of the country. The year following his reply to Mr. Hayne, he was invited by a large number of the most respectable citizens of New York and its vicinity, among whom were many distinguished gentlemen of both political parties, to meet them at a festival, offered to him as an expression of their great gratification at the course he had pursued in that memorable Constitutional contest. Chancellor Kent, who presided on the occasion, on addressing their guest, alluded in this felicitous manner to his speech : " It turned the attention of the public to the great doctrines of natural rights and national union. Constitutional law ceased to remain wrapped up in the breasts, and taught only by the responses, of the living oracles of the law. Socrates was said to have drawn philosophy from the skies, and scattered it among the schools. It may, with equal truth, be said, that Constitutional law, by means of these Senatorial discussions, and the master-genius that guided them, was rescued from the archives of our tribunals and the libraries of lawyers, and placed under the eye, and submitted to the judgment, of the American people. *Their verdict is with us, and from it there lies no appeal.*"

And another writer, hardly less eminent, Mr. Everett, has said of his arguments on the same, and later occasions: "The student of Constitutional law will ever resort to the speeches of Mr. Webster with the same deference that he pays to the numbers of the Federalist, and the opinions of Chief Justice Marshall. * * * The speech in reply to Mr. Calhoun and the speech on the Protest, are like leaves of the Constitution. They are authorities rather than illustrations. While we are engaged in perusing them, everything like mere discourse, however ingenious, forcible, or ornate, seems comparatively insipid."

With such demonstrations of public gratitude, and such expressions of warm encomium, were Mr. Webster's conduct and speeches on these two momentous occasions received throughout the country. All conceded to him ardent patriotism, incorruptible integrity, and unequalled ability. An emergency never arises without its accompanying and controlling spirit; and DANIEL WEBSTER seems to have been alone, of all the country, the man for each perilous crisis. But for him, Nullification, decorated and recommended by its two most ingenious and accomplished champions, might have seduced the affections of the people, and gained a permanent existence, to the inevitable disruption of the Union. But for him, our fathers' legacy, THE CONSTITUTION OF THE UNITED STATES—the great charter of political and social right—might have become a dishonored and worthless parchment. And but for him, constitutional and republican liberty—as it exists with us, the last hope of nations,—might have become a hissing and a reproach throughout the world. It was not without cause, then, that the country, with an almost univocal expression of its sentiment, greeted him with the title—prouder than monarch ever bestowed—of "Defender of the Constitution."

The wonderful interest felt in all of Mr. Webster's speeches springs from the language as well as the sentiment. A phrase often suggests abundant copiousness of thought; a word gives rise to feelings inexpressibly sweet or profound, like tunes in music; which recall times when freshness of heart was ours, ere bitter experience had belied the trustingness of earlier days. He borrows from no author, ancient or modern, either style or sentiment; and yet there is no speech of his not impregnated with the *afflatús divinus* of classical antiquity. The choicest productions of antiquity are fragrant of no flower which does not perfume his works; because his thought, like those of the antique world, is fresh, original, earnest, and finds correspondent articulation.

The encomium, which Quinctilian bestowed upon the philosophical writings of Brutus, "*Scias eum sentire quæ dicit*," you know that he *feels* what he says—applies with greater truth to Mr. Webster's works. He has felt himself what he makes us feel. His whole heart is in his language, and warms his page. This is the secret of its wonderful effect. The sacred historian informs us that "God gave Solomon largeness of heart;" and we need no other solution of the popularity of his writings, in every clime, from generation to generation. It requires a great heart to express a great truth. The learning of the schools cannot supply the want thereof; the wisdom of the wisest would strive in vain to make good its loss. To enrich the understanding, to stimulate or satisfy the ardent mind, is far easier than to gain the heart; one faculty can be acquired, the other is innate. You must be born an orator no less than a poet; for all of poetry is not rhythm, nor all of oratory language. There is something in both that eludes the most diligent and pertinacious analysis.

Compared with the productions of the most eminent orators of ancient or modern times, in what respect is the reply to Hayne inferior? In what production of ancient or modern times, shall we look for such a variety of genius? Where shall we find such majestic simplicity of expression, such beauty of illustration, such appropriateness of diction, where such ideal beauty of thought, embodied in such pleasing forms, where such gigantic power of reasoning, such depth of passion, such elevation of soul?

In tempestuous eloquence, which carries away in its ungoverned force, speaker no less than hearer, Demosthenes undoubtedly surpassed him; in carefully-elaborated periods, in equi-ponderance of sentences, in studied bursts of passion, as well as in general philosophy, Cicero excelled him. But what one work of either of those great masters of eloquence presents such a combination of various excellencies as the reply to Hayne? In what phillipic of either, or other immortal production, shall we look for its equal?

Of Modern Eloquence, we know nothing comparable. Much of Chatham depends upon tradition; more, perhaps, upon partial reporters; but, conceding to him all his most ardent admirers ever claimed, we still should deny him much reach of thought, or even well-sustained eloquence. Voice, manner, gesture, majesty of presence—all these he had; but all these produce but a temporary effect. His eloquence electrified rather than convinced; astonished more than it confuted; and mastered the passions rather than the judgment of men. It flashed like the lightning, which men gazed at with a fearful interest, ignorant of its direction; but once gone, the mind soon returned to its previous thought. His fame as an orator is the greater, that he left so little to sustain it. Contemporaneous opinion has been more favorable to him than faithful record might have been. No entire speech of his is extant; the fragmentary parts which we have, it is true, like the celebrated Torso of antiquity, reveal the possession of great genius, and forbid the hope of their completion by another hand. Still they afford no sufficient indication of what the merits of the whole would have been.

The philosophical orator of England—Edmund Burke—whose magnificent imagery, power of illustration, and vigor of thought have never been surpassed, was yet so warped by prejudice, was such a self-deluding sophist, as to leave no one production, not as much marred by great defects, as characterized by inimitable excellencies. In style, too, almost every work of his is as objectionable as in sentiment. He scatters, with a lavish hand, such a wasteful profusion of imagery, as to almost drown the sense of his meaning. The mind is puzzled, wearied by the accumulation of illustrations, and loses all command of the subject-matter. No one speech of this great writer, not the speech against Hastings, can hold the unwearied attention throughout.

There can be found in the speeches neither of Fox nor of his more distinguished rival—great Chatham's greater son—one, the equal to this of Mr. Webster's, in various merit. Fox exhibited at times more fiery declamation and more fervid eloquence; Pitt, more severity of invective and a wider range of argument; but neither, on any occasion, ever made a speech so complete in every point.

Brougham's speech on the Reform Bill, a masterly production doubtless, wants compactness of expression, and fidelity to the main question of debate, comparatively. But there are many passages of great eloquence in it, and its peroration is only inferior to Webster's.

The great charm of this speech, of all speeches of Mr. Webster, is the ardent patriotism and devotion to liberty that pervade them; a patriotism, not of a fanatical but universal character; not hating other countries from love of natal soil; but radiating from home a feeling of charity and good will upon all mankind; a devotion to liberty, as far removed from licentiousness as tyranny—liberty inseparable from virtue, from public and private morals—that imposes checks upon itself, and guards against the abuse of its own power.

It is this, which gives to his works their wide-spread popularity. It is this which has acclimated them everywhere. It is this which has carried the English language further than English arms have ever done; to regions of thick-ribbed ice, where day and night make one sad division of the year; to the utmost isles of the sea, and lands beyond the solar road.

He has spoken, and enslaved nations have started from the torpor of centuries. The down-trodden Greek has heard his voice, and risen upon his oppressors. The Turkish hordes have fallen where the Persian fell; and Marathon and Salamis shine with a newer glory, and a wider emblasonry.

As his words of cheering encouragement have crossed the equator and penetrated the southern seas, whole nations have thrown off the yoke of bondage, and achieved an independent existence. South America, emerging from beneath the horizon with its constellation of republics, has given light and gladness to the nations. His voice has called a New World into existence, to compensate for the decline of the old.*

* Englishmen give this praise to Canning, but hardly with as much

It is not yet hushed; his words have lost none of their vital force. The throes of Europe are their response. Subterranean fires are burning there with fatal activity; which burst out, ever and anon, in volcanic eruptions, overwhelming thrones, and destroying oppressors. It may not be long, ere one universal conflagration shall devour every vestige of tyranny, and liberated Europe spring up from the ruin, to recommence a more glorious career. and accomplish a surer destiny.

justice; for our country recognized the independence of the South American Republics before England.

CHAPTER XIII.

It was the fortune of General Jackson's administration to have provoked or undergone more public excitement, springing from causes of a domestic character, than that of either of his predecessors. A constant agitation pursued it throughout. The Hayne controversy roused the public mind from its apathetic state under the preceding administration, and stimulated it to apprehension and entertainment of elevated yet fearful themes. The war of nullification followed, ere the public pulse had recovered its accustomed tone, and gave a more turbulent motion to opinion. The passions excited by this quarrel had not subsided, but swayed the minds of men to and fro, as if tempest-tossed, when the Removal of the Deposites supervened, and raised the whole country.

The later history of the Bank of the United States may have reflected the necessity of this measure. Its subsequent mismanagement and explosion should, perhaps, be holden a retrospective justification of the decisive proceeding. But, at the time the removal of the deposites took place, the policy of the measure was not generally understood, while the immediate consequences thereof were everywhere felt, and felt disastrously.

It was no time for argument, however cogent; because no argument is listened to, when interest or passion speaks. That the powers of the Bank were too extensive, its immunities and privileges too unrestricted, few could now gainsay. Among the many dangerous powers enjoyed by this institution, the control over the contraction and expansion of the currency was not the least so. By the exercise of this power it could affect, to a most calamitous extent, the business of the whole nation. It was a power that existed not merely in theory, but had been felt in practice. In 1818–19, the directors of the institution availed themselves of its fatal character, to enrich themselves and friends, to the great calamity of the country; and, in 1831–32, to effect a political purpose, nearly thirty millions of loans were made in a few months, and called in again within as brief a time; great individual and national distress following the experiment. A power liable to such dangerous abuse should be checked, though at the hazard of temporary inconvenience.

The immediate consequence of General Jackson's decisive act was, undoubtedly, disastrous. The country was in a state of seeming prosperity, commercial and agricultural; but it was rather the hectic flush of consumption, than the color of robust health.

All kinds of operations had been stimulated by easy credits.

Every branch of business was pushed to its utmost extent, and stocks of every kind inflated, to near the limits of romance.

The withdrawal of eight millions from the bank, and the vindictive contraction of its issues by the bank, broke the bubble of speculation, and a collapse ensued. A severe pressure in the money market, the consequent high rate of interest, the depression of every kind of stock, and the low price of commodities, were the immediate results of these measures; and, no less, a strong, almost fierce agitation of the community.

The removal of the deposites took place in September, 1833; abont two months afterwards, in the greatest heat of the public feeling upon the subject, Congress met. The debates in that body are not only the safety valves of public excitement, but to an almost exclusive degree, the record of its existence. What might be otherwise as frail in memory as evanescent in feeling becomes, by incorporation in the proceedings of Congress, a permanent fact. Parliamentary action, with a free people, is a history of their sentiments, their wishes, and, too often, of their follies.

In the earliest of this session, Mr. Clay introduced a resolution into the Senate, calling upon the President for a copy of a paper said to have been read by him to the cabinet, in relation to the removal of the deposites, on the 18th of September preceding; which resolution he supported in an animated speech. It was carried, by a vote of twenty-three to eighteen. The State Rights men, who had not forgotten or forgiven General Jackson's decided course in the South Carolina controversy left the "Treasury Benches" in a body, and went over to the opposition; thereby reducing the strength of the administration in the Senate to a minority.

The answer of General Jackson to the resolution of the Senate was characteristic: "The Executive"—he said, in his communication to the Senate, "is a co-ordinate and independent branch of the Government equally with the Senate; and I have yet to learn under what constituted authority that branch of the legislature has a right to require of me an account of any communication, either verbally or in writing, made to the heads of departments acting as a cabinet-council. As well might I be required to detail to the Senate the free and private conversation I have held with those officers on any subjects relating to their duties and my own."

With this implied, if not direct, rebuke of the Senate for its unconstitutional interference in matters strictly executive, General Jackson declined compliance with the resolution.

His answer was received by the Senate with no demonstration of disrespectful anger; but in calmness and necessary acquiescence.

In the document which General Jackson submitted to his cabinet previous to the removal of the deposites—an official copy of which Mr. Clay had been unable to obtain for the Senate—he said: "The President deems it his duty to communicate in this manner to his cabinet, the final conclusions of his own mind, and the reasons on which they are founded;" and, in concluding his address to them, he said: "The President again repeats that he begs his cabinet to consider the proposed measure as *his own*, in support of which he shall require no one of them to make a sacrifice of opinion or principle. Its responsibility has been assumed, after the most mature deliberation and reflection, as necessary to preserve the morals of the people, the freedom of the press, and the purity of the elective franchise; without which, all will unite in saying that the blood and treasure expended by our forefathers, in the establishment of our happy system of government, will have been vain and fruitless." A fierce clamor was raised against the President for the communication of these sentiments, by the less moderate of the Opposition, in and out of Congress. They denounced him as an usurper of powers unrecognized by the Constitution; and charged upon him the intention of overthrowing the liberties of the country. Heated faction poured forth against him its choicest language of abuse, likening him to every variety of tyrant, lands most fertile in such products, ever nourished; so that many honest, though most credulous people, in different parts of the country, were sadly imposed upon. The fanaticism of party never achieved a more decided victory over sober truth.

But truth has this advantage over error; its conquests, if not so rapid, are permanent. And now that the delusion of the moment has passed away, with the excitement of which it was engendered, and reason has regained her sometime usurped authority, the conduct of General Jackson, in this menacing exigency of affairs, stands out boldly in the historical picture, reflecting courage, capacity, and marvellous foresight.

He was the man for a crisis. He feared nothing, he doubted nothing; he dared everything. He sought no evasion, he shunned no risk. He interposed no screen, no defence between himself and his enemies; but advancing to the very front of the battle, he defied them all: "I am here, who have done this thing; against me, against me, turn your weapons." He courted danger like a mistress.

He thought the deposites unsafe in the vaults of the bank, and removed them. He found the Secretary of the Treasury too timid to incur his share of the responsibility, and removed *him*. He knew what denunciation awaited him from rancorous opponents; what lukewarm support from timorous friends. He knew too his duty, and, heedless alike of fierce enmity or half-faced fellowship, dared perform it.

Not discouraged, though defeated in his first attack, Mr. Clay renewed his assaults upon the administration for its conduct in the matter of the public funds, with increased vigor. His indomitable courage and towering intellect, with his great Parliamentary tact, admirably qualified him for the post of leader, and made him no unworthy competitor of General Jackson himself. Foiled in one attack, he fell back, to assume a better position, and make defeat itself the handmaid of victory.

On the 26th of December, he offered in the Senate the following resolutions:

1. *Resolved*, That by dismissing the late Secretary of the Treasury, because he would not, contrary to his sense of his own duty, remove the money of the United States in deposit with the Bank of the United States and its branches, in conformity with the President's opinion, and by appointing his successor to effect such removal, which has been done, the President has assumed the exercise of a power over the Treasury of the United States, not granted to him by the Constitution and laws, and dangerous to the liberties of the people.

2. *Resolved*, That the reasons assigned by the Secretary of the Treasury for the removal of the money of the United States, deposited in the Bank of the United States, and its branches, communicated to Congress on the third day of December, 1833, are unsatisfactory and insufficient.

These resolutions Mr. Clay enforced in one of the strongest arguments of his life. He gave his whole heart to the speech. His burning eloquence carried away his audience, and loud plaudits from the gallery accompanied and interrupted him. These demonstrations of sympathy were of course immediately suppressed by the chair, who could not, however, prevent entirely their recurrence.

He passed from wit to argument, from satire to denunciation, "from lively to severe," with such rapidity that extremes seemed to touch, and laughter and indignation almost commingled. He put forth the whole variety of his intellect, omitting nothing, stinting nothing, exaggerating nothing.

His illustrations were peculiarly felicitous. The civil and loving expressions with which General Jackson ejected Mr. Duane—his recusant Secretary of the Treasury—reminded him, he said, of one of the most remarkable characters which our species has produced: "When Oliver Cromwell was contending for the mastery in Great Britain or Ireland, (I do not remember which,) he besieged a certain Catholic town. The place made a brave and stout resistance; but, at length, being likely to be taken, the poor Catholics proposed terms of capitulation, among which was one stipulating for the toleration of their religion. The paper containing the conditions being presented to Oliver, he put on his spectacles, and, after deliberately examining them, cried out, 'Oh, yes, granted, granted, certainly; but," he added with stern determination, "if one of them shall dare be found attending mass, he shall be instantly hanged."

There were many not less apposite than this, and some more illustrative of the points he made in his argument. He was listened to throughout with profound attention.

His speech was more argumentative than usual, less rhetorical. He seemed conscious that the importance of the controversy required all the skill in dialectics he could boast; and, with that admirable tact in the election of the proper style of oration which distinguishes him, he made a sound, logical, perspicuous argument; relieved, occasionally, it is true, with some ardent declamation, pungent satire, or brilliant fancy.

But, after all, Mr. Clay's style, whether of thought or manner, is not senatorial. It lacks dignity, elevation, gravity. His speech is often too colloquial, and even in some of its most effective passages, disfigured by provincialisms. He was never a scholar; has never studied those chaste models of style, the ancient classics, and, consequently knows, but imperfectly, how grandly to express a grand idea. The House of Representatives was the theatre of his greatness and his glory: there, his emphatic manner, his fervid eloquence, his earnest, though unchastened thought, gained him an admiration amounting almost to enthusiasm. Polish of style or accuracy of expression, was unnoticed or forgiven, in the *abandon* of feeling which his bold imagery, his vehement denunciation, and passionate appeals produced. As a popular speaker, he has had hardly an equal, certainly, no superior.

How different in manner, in thought, and in diction, Mr. Calhoun appeared! The fertile brevity of his expression, his power of thought, and the severe simplicity of his manner, placed him in violent contrast to his sometime rival. His speech had all the terseness of Tacitus, without his obscurity. It was illustrated more by axioms than imagery. Yet his language was so well-selected, so appropriate, so full of decorous words, that it required no other ornament.

He made a great argument on this occasion, saying more in two hours than almost any other Senator in two days. In the beginning, he defined his position: "I stand wholly disconnected with the two great political parties now contending for ascendancy. My political connections are with that small and denounced party, which has voluntarily wholly retired from the party strifes of the day, with a view of saving, if possible, the liberty and the Constitution of the country, in this great crisis of our affairs."

Alluding to the claim put forward by the friends of the administration, that in the removal of the deposites, it undertook to defend and guard the rights of States against the encroachments of the Federal Government, Mr. Calhoun spoke with unwonted energy. "The administration the guardians and defenders of the rights of the States! What shall I call it —audacity or hypocrisy? The authors of the proclamation, the guardians and defenders of the rights of the States! The authors of the war message against a member of this confederacy—the authors of the 'bloody bill'—the guardians and defenders of the rights of the States! This a struggle for State Rights! No, sir; State Rights are no more. The struggle is over for the present. The bill of the last session, which vested in the government the right of judging of the extent of its powers, finally and conclusively, and gave it the right of enforcing its judgment by the sword; destroyed all distinction between delegated and reserved rights; concentrated in the government the entire power of the system, and prostrated the States, as poor and helpless corporations, at the foot of this sovereignty."

His argument on this occasion was not disfigured by the painful abstractions of his usual speech. He held close to his subject, which he illustrated with great power. The mind of the audience followed him throughout.

Four times the space that measures day and night, did Mr. Benton address the Senate. The speech was an able one ; so much so, that his audience almost forgave him the want of ability to condense it. He left little of financial history or operations untouched ; and he commented upon little that he did not strengthen. Nor was it, to all minds, the least considerable merit of the speech that it allowed resting places to the attention. The distinguished orator would sometimes recapitulate—repeat in a variety of forms his argument—during which times the mind could recruit its somewhat exhausted force, and renew its capacity to apprehend. With Mr. Calhoun, on the contrary, there is no respite to the attention. The mind that would comprehend his argument, must listen to each word of his speech. Each sentence is so much dependent upon the preceding, that the loss of one link breaks the continuity of the argument, and mars the whole effect.

The great excitement prevailing in the country upon the removal of the deposites, was no where more intense than in the metropolis. Hither resorted persons from all sections of the country, most of whom, at this period, were violent partisans. The Senate-chamber was not saved from the ebulition of angry feeling, which exhibited itself sometimes in boisterous applause of one speaker, and sometimes in nerce condemnation of another. A tumultuous spirit threatened to overawe the Senate.

This spirit, so derogatory to the character of the Senate, and so revolutionary in its tendencies, the Vice-President, Mr. Van Buren, determined to put down. He warned the galleries to forbear all expression of opinion concerning matters in debate, or persons participating therein. Another violation of the respect due the Senate, he said, should be followed by the instant clearing of the galleries. To this end, he had instructed the officers of the Senate, who would take good care his orders were carried out. His determination of tone and manner quieted the crowd, who afterwards offered no interruption to the proceedings or debates of the Senate.

A model presiding officer was Mr. Van Buren. The attentive manner in which he listened, or seemed to listen, to each successive speaker, no matter how dull the subject, or how stupid the orator, the placidity of his countenance, unruffled in the midst of excitement, the modest dignity of his deportment, the gentlemanly ease of his address, his well-modulated voice and sympathetic smile, extorted admiration from even an opposing Senate ; while the proper firmness he displayed on all occasions, the readiness with which he met and repulsed any attack upon privileges or dignity of the Chair, the more conspicuous in contrast with the quiet indifference with which he entertained any merely personal assault, gained him the good will of all beholders.

He had served an apprenticeship to his high office by a senatorial career of six years, and qualified himself by the proper discharge of the duties of one position for the more responsible duties of the other. The peculiar delicacy and decorum which he had manifested during that term of service, in times of high party excitement, and in a decided minority, had won him great renown, and seemed to justify the general belief that he was intended for a larger sphere of action. Always self-controlled, he never uttered a word, direct or by inuendo, either from premeditation or in the heat of excitement, which need have wounded the feelings of a political opponent, in open or in secret session. Master of his own passions, he soon learnt to command those of other men. By study of himself, he acquired a knowledge of mankind. With a countenance always open, and thought always concealed, he invited without returning, confidence. Indeed, the character the great modern poet gives to one of his heroes will serve as an epitome, *mutatis mutandis*, of Mr. Van Buren's:

> " He was the mildest-mannered man,
> That ever scuttled ship or cut a throat;
> With such true feelings of the gentleman,
> You rarely could divine his real thought."

Virginia divided on this question of the removal of the deposites, as she had done on the Force Bill. Rives, now, as then, stood by the administration. Tyler contended both times, he said, for the Constitution. Rives made, perhaps, the strongest argument in defence of the President's policy, of the whole party. He was logical, candid, profound; and divided opinion even with Mr. Calhoun. As a constitutional argument, his effort deserved great praise. No one ever better explained the theory of executive power; strengthening his opinion, as he did, with the dicta of Madison, and other earliest and most eminent commentators of the Constitution. He denied that General Jackson had transcended the constitutional limits of his office, in the removal of the deposites, and compelled the Opposition to fall back upon the impolicy and abruptness of that proceeding. His speech on the Force Bill had given a promise of excellence which this more than confirmed.

Nor did his colleague, Mr. Tyler, make an indifferent speech. He hauled closer to the wind than usual, and lost less time and less power in unnecessary diversions. He spoke with much animation and earnestness of manner. "We are told," he said, "of the great power of the Bank, sir; is there no danger from power in any other direction? Are gentlemen blind to the power of the President? In its mildest form it is immense; look into the Blue Book; count up the number of his retainers—of those who live only by his smile, and perish by his frown—here are forty thousand public officers of the government. The Dukes of Burgundy, who agitated Europe in the time of the Henrys of England and the Philips and Louises of France, could not count so many. The Earl of

Warwick, the king-maker of England, had not one fourth so many." Power, it is said, corrupts its possessor. Of this, the Syrian, who, yet unused to it, replied incredulously and indignantly to the prophet, as he predicted the enormities of his coming reign—"Is thy servant a dog, that he should do these things?" is not the sole historical illustration. Little did the orator think, on this occasion, while he fulminated against the abuse of power by General Jackson, how soon he should be subjected to its dangerous exercise. If he went through the ordeal, with less of self-reproach or public opprobrium than he whose conduct he so strongly reprobated, history will mitigate its damnatory records of gross abuse of power with one instance of glorious self-control.

Mr. Rives' speech on this occasion cost him his seat in the Senate. The Legislature of Virginia, with the petty intolerance that distinguishes the ignorant, "instructed" him out of it—the only kind of instruction, perhaps, it was in its power to render him. His rebound, however, was greater than his fall; for, soon after, he was called upon by the President, to exert, for the benefit of his country, in an eminent position abroad, those rare qualities which the ingratitude of his State would not suffer him to display in a subordinate position at home. He avenged himself upon his State, which refused his service, by enhancing the glory of her name, and promoting the prosperity of the country, which, on her ostracism, had adopted him.

Much agitation, all the while the debate was going on,

excited the mind of General Jackson. As reports of speeches were daily made to him, he betrayed more or less emotion according to their character. He spoke in terms somewhat objurgatory of Mr. Clay's speech; of Mr. Calhoun's, in terms decidedly so. In truth, a reservation of his sentiments was not a common fault with General Jackson. It might rather have been complained, that the language in which he gave them utterance was sometimes too strong, too vehement, too personal. It was illustrated with expressions that had been better omitted. "Our army swore terribly in Flanders;" and it is not to be disguised, that General Jackson transferred to civil life the habit he acquired in camps, of too energetic epithets. It was, however, only in moments of great excitement, when reason is, as it were, for a time in abeyance, that he indulged in a habit so reprehensible in a gentleman, so unbecoming, and, from example, so pernicious, in the highest officer of the government.

But for Mr. Calhoun, General Jackson, at this time, entertained a theological hatred. Ordinary language, he feared, could not give it adequate revelation. It must be characterized, he thought, by language no less decided than itself. It could not find vent in hostile action, or he would have gratified it otherwise than in words. Words were the only outlet to his anger, and he selected the most expressive.

General Jackson felt a stronger personal interest in this debate than in the debate upon the Force Bill. In that more important interests were agitated, but none to affect him personally so near. The defeat of his recommendations on that occasion, would, undoubtedly, very materially, have weakened the moral force of his administration, if it had not destroyed it wholly; but the personal consequences might not have been so disastrous as they threatened to be in this. The responsibility of his action, on that occasion, was shared by his cabinet, by the larger portion of his own party, and by the almost unanimous strength of the Opposition, and applauded by the country generally. Had he failed of success, the sympathy in his favor would, in a very short period, have even added to his already formidable popularity, and temporary discomfiture been succeeded by permanent and almost illimitable power.

But the removal of the deposites he had assumed as his own act. He had relieved, by open proclamation, his cabinet from any participation in it. It was an act, he well knew, which many of his friends hesitated to defend, while it rendered a fierce opposition still fiercer. Nor was the country generally, he could not but feel, as on the former occasion, disposed to warmly concur in his action. A panic seized the financial and commercial interests, and affected, indeed, more or less disastrously, every class of the community; a panic encouraged and exaggerated by the retaliatory measures of the Bank, so that an entire stagnation of all trade and operations seemed inevitable.

The passage of these resolutions by the Senate of the United States, a majority of whom were his former political friends, could not, he thought, but prove injurious to his administration.

It would be the first check, of any important character, it had ever encountered, since its commencement. The act would go forth to the world as a grave, authoritative, official condemnation of his conduct. It would lessen the magic influence of his name, in destroying the belief in its invincibility, and might draw after it consequences alike disastrous to his administration and the party. To prevent the passage of the resolutions, therefore, was his first hope; and, failing in that, the next was, to give them such a character and intent, as to render them incapable of injury to himself, with the country.

From the Nullifiers, or State Rights party, in the Senate, General Jackson looked for no support. He knew there were no harsher enemies than warm friends alienated; and his former intimacy with that party prepared him for its vindictive opposition now. But there were in the Senate three or four of no determined purpose, whose action awaited the superior argument, or most conclusive reasons, of one side or the other. With as much integrity as the rest of the Senate, they had not been able to come to so early conclusion in regard to the policy of censuring General Jackson's proceedings. Their votes would decide the contest, and consequently there was an eager struggle on both sides to obtain them.

Mr. Clay's resolution of censure originally read: *Resolved*, That by dismissing the late Secretary of the Treasury, because he would not, contrary to his sense of his own duty, remove the money of the United States, in deposit with the Bank of the United States and its branches, in conformity with the President's opinion ; and by appointing his successor to effect such removal, which has been done, the President has assumed the exercise of a power over the Treasury of the United States not granted to him by the Constitution and laws, and dangerous to the liberties of the people."

This resolution specified certain acts of the President, which it denounced as a violation of the Constitution and laws. The particular conclusion of fact or law, which induced any Senator to vote for it, would appear from the very terms of the resolution.

The mover of the resolution, discovered during the debate, and particularly after the arguments of Mr. Rives and Mr. Forsyth, that, unless modified, it would probably fail—the moderates declining to vote for it. He therefore modified it, as follows :

"*Resolved*—That in taking upon himself the responsibility of removing the deposites of the public money from the Bank of the United States, the President of the United States has assumed the exercise of a power over the Treasury of the United States, not granted to him by the Constitution and laws, and dangerous to the liberties of the people."

This resolution, thus amended, he offered to the Senate towards the close of the debate. It still did not satisfy the scrupulous party, who held the balance of power between the two extremes. The able and legal argument of Mr. Wright, of New York, the last that was made on the side of the friends of the administration, threatened to secure the rejection of the resolution, even in its amended form.

The politic leader of the opposition, always full of resources, and always ready to concede to tender consciences whatever would not interfere with the prospect of triumph, again modified his resolution, making it read thus:

"*Resolved*—That the President, in the late executive proceedings in relation to the public revenue, has assumed upon himself authority and power not conferred by the Constitution and laws, but in derogation of both."

The character of these changes was important. The first omitted the specification on which the general charge against the President of having violated the Constitution and laws depended, but still retained the clause that accused him of conduct "dangerous to the liberties of the people." The second change not only omitted the specification, but the impeaching clause—"dangerous to the liberties of the people"—besides. These changes were decisive of the vote. The resolution of censure finally passed on the 28th of March, 1834, by a vote of twenty-six to twenty; eight of the twenty-six having been original Jackson-men.

The other resolution of Mr. Clay, declaring the reasons assigned by the Secretary of the Treasury for the removal of the deposites insufficient, passed by a vote of twenty-eight to eighteen.

In the acrimonious debate upon this occasion, Mr. Webster took no part. He could not approve the act of the President in removing the deposites, yet would not join those who seized this opportunity of making a personal attack upon him. He could not but recollect that a few short months before, the President and himself were upon terms of cordiality—that they had reciprocated mutual kindnesses ; and he was not prepared so early to forego such grateful reminiscences, and adopt, instead of friendly courtesies, the language of denunciation and menace. To others, he left the invidious task of impunging the motives and arraigning the character of General Jackson ;—for himself, he was content to record a silent and respectful dissent to this measure of his administration.

But the passage of Mr. Clay's resolutions exasperated rather than allayed the division between the Executive and Senate. To the vote of censure passed upon his act by the Senate, Gen. Jackson sent to that body, on the 17th April, 1834, his memorable PROTEST. The resolution of the Senate, he said, was in substance an impeachment of the President ; and, in its passage, amounted to a declaration, by the majority of the Senate, that he was guilty of an impeachable offence. As such it was spread upon the journals of the Senate—published to the nation and the world,—made part of our enduring archives—and incorporated in the history of the age.

The Constitution makes the House of Representatives the exclusive judges, in the first instance, of the question, whether the President has committed an impeachable offence. But, according to the argument of the President, a majority of the

Senate, whose interference with this preliminary question had been studiously excluded, anticipated the action of the House of Representatives, and not only assumed the function that belongs exclusively to that body, but converted themselves into accusers, witnesses, counsel and judges.

The argument of the Protest was most ingenious, and highly creditable to its distinguished author. He defended, with great force of logic, two positions: 1st. That the Executive, under the constitution and the laws, was the sole custodian of the public funds ; and 2dly, that even on the supposition the President had assumed an illegal power in the removal of the deposites, the Senate had no right, by resolution, in that or any other case, to express disapprobation of the President's conduct. He was amenable to the action of neither House of Congress, unless by the constitutional method of impeachment.

The introduction of the Protest into the Senate opened wide again the flood-gates of debate. All who had spoken before plunged in now, and some with greater vehemence. The excitement in the Senate was intense, and occasionally irrepressible. Mr. Leigh, of Va., concluding a speech, with a glowing encomium upon Mr. Clay for his services in getting through the tariff compromise act of 1833, "brought down" the galleries. The cheering and mingled hisses were so violent, that the Vice-President ordered the galleries to be cleared; and while the sergeant-at-arms was proceeding in the execution of the order, the noise and disturbance became yet more outrageous. Some names were vociferated, with tumultuous approbation—others, with as vehement vituperation; and, among the latter, the name of the President. This excited the indignation of Col. Benton, who moved that "the Bank-ruffians" that had committed the outrage should be taken into custody, accompanying his motion with remarks emphatically condemnatory of the rioters. Mr. Moore, of Ala., thought the motion unnecessary, as it could not be carried out. The whole gallery must be arrested, or no one—for it was impossible to distinguish, amid so much confusion, the innocent from the guilty. But Mr. Benton, with some warmth, insisted on his motion, upon which he demanded the ayes and noes; and they were ordered accordingly.

Mr. Clayton, as soon as he could make himself heard beyond the noise on the floor as well as in the galleries, regretted the motion had been made, but since it had been, he should vote against it. He did not regard the disturbance as an intended contempt of the Senate, but only as an indiscreet expression of public opinion.

Mr. Benton replied, that the terms in which he expressed his motion were so distinct as not to be misunderstood. He would not be misunderstood. He did not move to take into custody those, who, in an unguarded moment, had applauded the sentiments of the Senator from Virginia, but those, who, long after the gentleman had taken his seat, had continued to outrage and insult the Senate.

While motions were made to adjourn, and to lay Col.

Benton's motion on the table, the chair pronouncing them severally out of order, the galleries became cleared. The Senate then assumed a more pacific aspect, and order was recovered. Mr. Benton withdrew his motion, because the galleries being all cleared, he said, there was no one upon whom it could operate.

While the debate maintained a personal character, and seemed used but as an opportunity for the display of angry feeling on either side, Mr. Webster continued silent. His object was to discourage, not to foment, prejudices—to mitigate and not to exasperate passions already dangerously excited; and it was not till men's minds had been brought, mostly by his example and remonstrance, to a temperature susceptible of dispassionate argument, that he arose to address the Senate.

In his exordium, he spoke of the President in the language of respect—from which he did not deviate in any part of his argument: "Unhappily, sir, the Senate finds itself involved in a controversy with the President of the United States; a man who has rendered most distinguished services to his country, has hitherto possessed a degree of popular favor perhaps never excelled, and whose honesty of motive and integrity of purpose are still maintained by those who admit that his administration has fallen into lamentable errors."

Thus, while persons, once his friends, were assailing Gen. Jackson's motives and ferociously denouncing his policy, Mr. Wesbster, never other than his political opponent, always conceded the honesty of his intentions even when compelled by his convictions to oppose his measures.

The Senate—he said in this speech—regarded the direct interposition of the President in the removal of the deposites, as an interference with the legislative disposition of the public treasure. Every encroachment, great or small, was important enough to awaken the attention of those who were intrusted with the preservation of a Constitutional Government. It was in this relation that he expressed his thoughts in sentences that have been pronounced some of the most beautiful and energetic, in any of his works. Speaking of the resistance made by our ancestors to the assertion of the right of Parliament to tax them, he said: "It was against the recital of an act of Parliament, rather than any suffering under its enactments, that they took up arms. They went to war against a preamble. They fought seven years against a declaration. They poured out their treasures and their blood like water, in a contest in opposition to an assertion which those less sagacious, and not so well schooled in the principles of civil liberty, would have regarded as barren phraseology, or mere parade of words. They saw in the claim of the British Parliament a seminal principle of mischief, the germ of unjust power; they detected it, dragged it forth from underneath its plausible disguises, struck at it; nor did it elude their steady eye, or their well directed blow, till they had extirpated and destroyed it to the smallest fibre. On this question of principle, while actual suffering was yet afar off, they raised their flag against a power, to which, for purposes of foreign conquest and subjugation, Rome, in the height of her glory, is not to be compared—a power which has dotted over the surface of the whole globe with her possessions and military posts, whose morning drum-beat, following the sun, and keeping company with the hours, circles the earth daily with one continuous and unbroken strain of the martial airs of England."

In reply to the claim of the President, that the Executive had the sole control of the public funds, Mr. Webster said in his argument: "Mr. President, the Executive claim of power is exactly this, that the President may keep the money of the public in whatever banks he chooses, on whatever terms he chooses, and to apply the sums which those banks are willing to pay for its use to whatever purposes he chooses. These sums are not to come into the general treasury. They are to be appropriated before they get there; they are never to be brought under the control of Congress; they are to be paid to officers and agents not known to the law, not nominated to the Senate, and responsible to nobody but the Executive itself. I ask gentlemen if all this be lawful? Are they prepared to defend it? Will they stand up and justify it? In my opinion, sir, it is a clear and most dangerous assumption of power. It is the creation of office without law; the appointment to office without consulting the Senate; the establishment of a salary without law; and the payment of that salary out of a fund which itself is derived from the use of the public treasures."

In truth, the argument of Mr. Webster on this point concludes the question; and leaves the act of the President to the defensive plea of necessity—a necessity clear, cogent, and imperative; that admitted of no delay, and tolerated no alternative. It was upon this ground alone that his friends finally defended it; and upon this alone will it generally be held defensible by posterity.

The other argument of the Protest that the Senate had no right to express disapprobation of the President's conduct, Mr. Webster combatted, with brief but emphatic logic. "We need not look far," he said, "nor look deep, for the foundation of this right in the Senate. It is clearly visible and close at hand. In the first place, it is the right of self-defence. In the second place, it is a right founded on the duty of representative bodies, in a free government, to defend the public liberty against encroachment. We must presume that the Senate honestly entertained the opinion expressed in the resolution of the 28th of March; and, entertaining that opinion, its right to express it is but a necessary consequence of its right to defend its own constitutional authority, as one branch of the Government. This is its clear right, and this, too, is its imperative duty.

* * * * * *

The Senate has acted not in its judicial, but in its legislative capacity. As a legislative body, it has defended its own just authority, and the authority of the other branch of the Legislature. Whatever attacks our own rights or privileges, or whatever encroaches on the power of both Houses, we may oppose and resist, by declaration, resolution, or other similar proceedings. If we look to the books of precedents, if we examine the journals of legislative bodies, we find everywhere instances of such proceedings."

The speech on the Protest, received a no less distinguished and ardent reception in the country generally, than the speeches in reply to Hayne, and on the Force Bill. Equally with these, it responded to the dominant sentiment of the people. Persons of all political opinions, and of various pursuits, addressed Mr. Webster thanks for the effort. Some of the most eminent jurists and statesmen of the nation proferred him their warmest approbation;—among whom were Chancellor Kent of New York, and Littleton W. Tazewell of Virginia; differing on most subjects of constitutional law, they agreed fully upon this. "I had just finished," writes Chancellor Kent to Mr. Webster some days after the speech was delivered, "the rapturous perusal of your speech on the Protest as appearing in the Intelligencer of Saturday, when I had the pleasure of receiving it from you in a pamphlet form. I never had a greater treat than the reading of that speech this morning. You never equalled this effort. It surpasses everything in logic—in simplicity and beauty and energy of diction—in clearness—in rebuke—in sarcasm—in patriotic and glowing feelings—in just and profound constitutional views—in critical severity and matchless strength. It is worth millions to our liberties."

And Gov. Tazewell, writing to Mr. Tyler says: "Tell Webster from me that I have read his speech in the National Intelligencer, with more pleasure than any I have lately seen. If the approbation of it by one who has not been used to coincide with him in opinion can be grateful to him, he has mine *in extenso.* I agree with him perfectly, and thank him cordially for his many excellent illustrations of what I always thought. If it is published in pamplet form, beg him to send me one. I will have it bound in good Russia leather, and will leave it as a special legacy to my children."

That the merits of this speech as a constitutional argument should have been so earnestly impressed upon two persons of such distinguished and yet diverse opinions in relation to constitutional questions, is no ordinary proof of its profound truthfulness. For while sophistry presents many phases, and is viewed in various and changeful light, truth, to the thoughtful and sagacious, has but one aspect, and is immutable. The argument on the Protest, as the exposition of sound, patent, constitutional doctrine, has its equal nowhere—not even in any previous or subsequent effort of Mr. Webster himself.

These three great speeches of Mr. Webster,—the Reply to Hayne, the speech on the Force Bill, and upon the Protest—are, most undoubtedly, the best exposition of constitutional law ever given to the country. They constitute a chart of government. And, as in the ancient days of Rome, the magistrates, whenever danger pressed the eternal city, consulted the Sybilline Books, to know what measures of safety to pursue, so, under our government, with us, and with posterity, these inspired productions of his great mind, in time of peril to the Constitution and the Union, will ever be resorted to as the only hope or means of preservation. By their saving guidance, THE CONSTITUTION AND THE UNION, "one and inseparable," may survive every storm, and ride victorious through every gale.

Attachment to the Union of the States has amounted with Mr. Webster to a passion. It was his earliest love and will endure to his latest breath. In whatever situation he has been placed, it has filled his heart and controlled his conduct. He was made everything, in public life, subsidiary to this. It has grown with his growth, and strengthened with his strength, till it has become a part of his moral being.

The past is security for the future—no matter how much his motives may be arraigned, his conduct vilified, or his personal feelings outraged, he will maintain, steadfast and unshaken, his devotion to the Constitution and the Union. He will neither forego nor qualify that ardent devotion, at the instigation of angry clamor, or be diverted a hair's-breadth from his consistent course, by the frowns or smiles of power, whether centered in one man or the million. He knows no change. He takes no step backwards, whatever denunciation or whatever blandishments surround him, he will be true, whoever else is faithless. As well might we expect the NORTH STAR,—in all time, that unsubsidized guide to the mariner,—to withhold his light and refuse to shine, because the needle, with fickle polarity, inclines to some other luminary.

"I am," he says now as he said before, "where I have ever been, and ever mean to be. Standing on the platform of the general Constitution—a platform, broad enough, and firm enough, to uphold every interest of the whole country—I shall still be found. Intrusted with some part in the administration of that Constitution, I intend to act in its spirit and in the spirit of those who framed it. I would act as if our fathers who formed it for us, and who bequeathed it to us, were looking on me—as if I could see their venerable forms bending down to behold us from the abodes above. I would act too as if the eye of posterity was gazing on me.

"Standing thus, as in the full gaze of our ancestors and our posterity, having received this inheritance from the former, to be transmitted to the latter, and feeling that, if I am formed for any good, in my day and generation, it is for the good of the whole country, no local policy or local feeling, no temporary impulse, shall induce me to yield my foothold on the Constitution and the Union.

"I came into public life in the service of the United States. On that broad altar, my earliest, and all my public vows, have been made. I propose to serve no other master. So far as depends on any agency of mine, they shall continue United States; united in interest and affection; united in everything in regard to which the Constitution has decreed their union; united in war, for the common defence, the common renown, and the common glory; and united, compacted, knit firmly together in peace, for the common prosperity and happiness of ourselves and our children."

www.ingramcontent.com/pod-product-compliance
Lightning Source LLC
LaVergne TN
LVHW020242110826
845151LV00003B/1012